Guide for Developing and Evaluating
School Library Programs

The Nebraska Guide for Developing and Evaluating School Library Programs Mission Statement

The school library program provides access to information and ideas for the entire school community and is an integral component in the total educational process for student learning. This is a mission accomplished through partnerships among school librarians, teachers, students, administrators, family and the community members as they plan and establish the goals for the school library program. The program is then implemented and directed by the certificated school librarian in their role as teacher, leader, information specialist, instructional partner, and program administrator.

> —American Association of School Librarians, *Empowering Learners: Guidelines for School Library Media Programs* (2009, p. 16)

Project Coordinator: Deborah Levitov, *School Library Monthly*, Libraries Unlimited

Publication Committee Members:

Laurie Bauer
Bayard Public Schools

Phyllis Brunken
Educational Service Unit 7 (retired)

Jackie Davis
Hastings Public School

Mary Ellis
*McDaid Elementary and St. Patrick
High Schools*

nack
chools

Rebecca J. Pasco
University of Nebraska–Omaha

Laura Pietsch
Bellevue Public Schools

Marilyn Scahill
Millard Public Schools

Joie Taylor
Columbus Public Schools (retired)

Susan Vanneman
Lincoln Public Schools (retired)

Ruth Walker
Mitchell Public Schools

Karla Wendelin
Lincoln Public Schools (retired)

Sandy White
Educational Service Unit 13

Glenda Willnerd
Lincoln Public Schools

Guide for Developing and Evaluating School Library Programs

Seventh Edition

Nebraska Educational Media Association

Santa

Library of Congress Cataloging-in-Publication Data

Guide for developing and evaluating school library programs / Nebraska Educational Media Association. — 7th ed.

   cm.

Guide for developing and evaluating school library media d. 2000.

phical references and index.

7-0 (acid-free paper)

ka.   2. Instructional materials centers—Nebraska.

—Evaluation.   4. Instructional materials

I. Nebraska Educational Media Association.

ing school library media programs.

an eBook.

Contents

Preface

The publication of a guide for school library programs in Nebraska began with the original *Guide for Evaluating, Establishing, and Developing School Media Programs*, written in 1973. It was edited in 1974 to become the *Nebraska Guide for Establishing, Developing, and Evaluating School Media Programs*. Since this second edition did not reflect the national standards, another update of the Nebraska guide, *Media Programs: District and School*, coauthored in 1975 by the Association for Educational Communications and Technology (AECT) and the American Association of School Librarians (AASL), was undertaken in 1982; this was the third edition.

Several years later, in 1990, a fourth revision of the guide was undertaken to respond to the many technological developments and continuous educational changes that were influencing school library media programs across the state. The new edition was also needed to reflect the 1988 national AECT-AASL standards, *Information Power: Guidelines for School and Media Programs*. Though previous national standards had, for the most part, gone unnoticed by the educational community, the impact of *Information Power* was dramatic, and the *Nebraska Guide* became an important publication for school library media programs in Nebraska as they worked to implement the national standards.

The 1994 *Nebraska Guide*, the fifth revision, was published to provide updated information and better assist Nebraska school librarians as they developed exciting and effective programs that were integrated into existing curricula.

In 1998 new national standards, *Information Power: Building Partnerships for Learning*, were published by AECT-AASL. These standards modeled and emphasized the importance of information literacy instruction in addition to the key role of collaborative partnerships among school librarians, teachers, administrators, students, and the entire learning community in the development of effective library media programs. This again established the need for a sixth edition of the *Nebraska Guide* to be correlated with the new *Information Power* standards: *The Guide for Developing and Evaluating School Library Media Programs* (2000).

In 2007 AASL published the *Standards for the 21st-Century Learners* and in 2009 published updated guidelines for school libraries, *Empowering Learners: Guidelines for School Library Media Programs*. Thus this is the publication of the seventh edition of the guide by the Nebraska Educational Media Association (NEMA) and the second edition published with Libraries Unlimited. It is aligned to the new program guidelines and learning standards of AASL. The intent is to create a guide that will be useful to all school librarians nationwide and to other educators, providing a foundation for the continued development of school library programs as they strive to meet the challenges of all persons living, learning, and working in the 21st century.

Grateful recognition goes to the many dedicated NEMA members who helped edit and update this edition of the guide.

Introduction

The school library of the 21st century is student centered, meeting the needs of all learners. It serves as a safe haven for students, providing a comfortable and inviting gathering place for learning and studying as well as a place for pursuing personal growth. The school library provides an appropriate balance of digital and textual resources with differentiated instruction central to educational planning for developing 21st-century skills.

The realization of a dynamic 21st-century school library program requires a school librarian who is a skilled teacher and program administrator, a creative risk taker, and a transformative leader with a vision for the school library program. As an accomplished user of technology and a lifelong learner with expertise as an information specialist, the school librarian serves as an information and inquiry expert. The school librarian assists students in their pursuit of information and knowledge as they use necessary multiple literacy skills and resources in all formats. The school librarian must be an instructional partner who is approachable, collaborative, flexible, adaptable, and capable of dovetailing many tasks.

The purpose of this guide is to assist schools in the realization of school libraries that meet the needs of the 21st-century learner. It makes available information for developing and/or improving school library programs and provides qualitative and quantitative criteria for assessing library programs. Its intent is to meet the needs of diverse school systems nationwide and give direction for implementing school library programs while offering a viable evaluation tool. A major focus of this revision is to provide a plan that emphasizes the individual needs of each school for its school library, students, and teachers. The guide stresses that successful implementation requires that the school librarian form a partnership that involves students, teachers, administrators, and families and makes links to the community.

The *Guide for Developing and Evaluating School Library Programs* includes seven basic chapters: (1) "Leadership for School Library Program Development," (2) "Preparation of School Library Professionals," (3) "Preparation and Training of School Library Paraprofessionals," (4) "School Library Personnel and Evaluation," (5) "Teaching for Learning and the School Library Program," (6) "Collection Development: Managing School Library Resources," and (7) "School Library Facilities."

The seventh edition of this guide (the sixth edition was also published with Libraries Unlimited) has been accomplished through the efforts of Nebraska school librarians representing public and private schools, colleges, universities, and Educational Service Units in Nebraska.

INSTRUCTIONS FOR USE

This guide may be used as a complete unit for program evaluation or for evaluation by an outside agency. It may be used as a whole to guide the development of a school library program or in segments to assess the separate factors of a library program.

The guide includes a rationale and instructions for use for each chapter. Although the approach to each of the seven chapters may often be different and distinct, there is a common thread of purpose and a common philosophy that bind the seven together and link them to the national standards, *Empowering Learners: Guidelines for School Library Media Programs*, published by the American Association of School Librarians (2009).

1

Leadership for School Library Program Development

RATIONALE

To realize the goals and objectives for school library programming outlined in the national guidelines developed by the American Association of School Librarians (AASL 2009b), *Empowering Learners: Guidelines for School Library Media Programs*, school librarians must have strong leadership skills and strategies for adept planning and management. The intent of this chapter is to provide tools and resources that will help guide the school librarian in developing leadership capacity and strategies that involve collaborating with others in the development of an effective school library program and facilitating ongoing program evaluation.

To begin the process of program planning, school librarians must first identify and internalize a philosophy for the school library program. They must then develop leadership skills so that they can communicate and model a clear understanding of the vision presented in *Empowering Learners* (AASL 2009b), promote the potential of the school library program, and establish credibility. With strong leadership skills, school librarians can work to build partnerships between administrators, faculty, students, parents, and the community in relationship to the school library program. Advocacy and public relations for school libraries must be an outcome of these leadership efforts. Through the establishment of educational partnerships, the concepts that are central to school libraries related to information access, information literacy, use of technology, and a focus on the inquiry process can be connected across all curricular areas. As a result, a student-centered, learning-focused school library program can be realized, putting students and their educational needs at the heart of the program.

Technology is essential to teaching and learning as well as managing and organizing library resources and services of the 21st century. The school librarian must be central to the planning process for effective use of technology, serving as a leader in helping students and teachers as well as others in the learning community gain awareness of and competency in the use of relevant technological resources. Information literacy and inquiry are key components to integrating technology throughout the educational process.

Collaboration is central to developing objectives for the planning, management, and evaluation of the library program while creating educational connections to resources and information literacy. Planning involves the leadership of the school librarian as he or she works collaboratively with others to define the mission, goals, objectives, and policies of the school library program and then communicate them effectively. Program planning and evaluation are ongoing, systematic processes that promote the achievement of current goals and allow a response to new trends in education and technological advancement. As a result, the school library program will be an established part of the academic goals of the school and will be part of school improvement planning—serving the school community as a program that adapts, evolves, and changes with educational needs and demands.

Through leadership the program is guided; through collaboration a joint mission is established; through advocacy essential partnerships are created and sustained; and through technology an effective program is organized and facilitated for teaching and learning.

To remain knowledgeable of current changes in education, technology, and library and information sciences, the school librarian must pursue available professional development opportunities that assist in developing and enhancing the roles of leader, instructional partner, information specialist, teacher, and program administrator (AASL 2009b, 16). The school librarian must also be active in promoting opportunities for students, teachers, and others in the learning community to acquire new skills related to information literacy and technology.

INSTRUCTIONS FOR USE

This chapter has four components. The first addresses an overview of planning and implementation of *Empowering Learners: Guidelines for School Library Media Programs* (AASL 2009b), and the second focuses on advocacy and leadership for the school library program. The third part provides ideas and tools for evaluating the school library program at different levels and from various perspectives. The fourth part provides a checklist plan for professional development for the school librarian. In addition, an extensive list of resources is included at the end of the chapter.

PLANNING AND IMPLEMENTATION OF EMPOWERING LEARNERS

The materials in this section may be used in planning, implementing, and sustaining *Empowering Learners: Guidelines for School Library Media Programs* (AASL 2009b). To assist in implementation, additional resources may be accessed through the American Association of School Librarians Web site (http://www.ala.org/aasl) as well as through other professional journals and publications.

The planning process is a continuous, collaborative effort. "Only through the development of an articulated mission and long-range plan will school librarians be able to implement an effective school library program that positively impacts student achievement. By continuously reflecting on our progress and retooling as necessary, school librarians can lead the way in building a learning environment that supports development of the skills learners need to be active members of our global society" (AASL 2009b, 48).

Empowering Learners: Guidelines for School Library Media Programs (AASL 2009b) contains the following key concepts that shape the school library program:

- Teaching and learning are central to the school library program.

- Collaboration is a key element.

- A technology-rich environment is essential.

- A multitude of varied resources is necessary.

- Access and availability to resources must be 24-7.

In addition to these key concepts, to develop a strong school library program, the five roles of the school librarian must be developed and put into practice:

- leader

- instructional partner

- information specialist

- teacher

- program administrator (AASL 2009b, 17–18)

An understanding of the key concepts and roles must be adhered to through program development, and essential to that is the development of a mission statement.

Mission Statements

A mission statement is a concise expression of the purpose of an organization or program that specifies the fundamental reasons for its existence. "It is important that the school library program requires students to be critical thinkers, adept problem solvers, and fluent and respectful communicators" (Zmuda 2007, 24–26). The key concepts should be part of the mission statement, which reflects the mission of the school.

When developing the mission statement for the school library program, the following should be considered. The school library program mission statement should

- reflect the school's mission statement

- reflect the core purpose and image of the school library program

- indicate how the school library program mission supports student achievement

- identify the stakeholders, taking into account both current and future needs

- consist of at least 25 words but not more than 75 words

- use broad and general terms

Mission Statement Samples

The AASL mission statement for the school library program follows: "The mission of the school library media program is to ensure that students and staff are effective users of ideas and information" (AASL 2009b, 8).

District Mission Statement

"The mission of the Lincoln Public Schools Library Media Services Department is to provide a facility and program to empower the 21st-century learner with the ability to access and process information and ideas and to support the educational goals of the school community."

Building Library Media Center Mission Statement

"Robin Mickle Media Center seeks to provide an environment that enables middle school learners and their teachers to access, evaluate, and use information relevant to their school needs and of interest to them in their personal lives. It strives to prepare learners to live in a diverse, technological world."

Leadership

A school librarian as a leader facilitates the development of strong library programs to affect student achievement. The qualities of the school librarian leader include, but are not limited to, the following: passionate innovator, consensus builder, collaborator, professional learner, connector, advocate, visionary, change agent.

Leadership of the school library program is critical to the process of program planning and implementation. To be a leader, the school librarian must

- carry the vision
- organize a clearly defined planning timeline
- identify objectives
- provide ways to collect needed information and data
- identify target groups
- prepare implementation strategies for recommendations
- plan for communication
- set up a regular evaluation process
- be a proponent for the process
- be an advocate for the program
- recruit advocates for the program

Under the leadership of the school librarian, it is helpful to have a planning committee composed of various representatives from stakeholder groups (e.g., teachers, administrators, students, parents, community members). This committee can help plan, implement, and retool program development, as necessary, to ensure an effective program. It can also be a vehicle for the school librarian in developing advocates for the school library program who understand its mission and will speak out on behalf of the program and the school librarian.

The following worksheet can be used in planning for and implementing *Empowering Learners* (AASL 2009b).

Table 1.1 School Library Advocacy Planning Worksheet

Date: Project No.:

Objective(s)

Target Group(s)—Focus on the decision makers; other groups may be part of your strategy.

Note: Use a different planning sheet for each target group you identify.

Strategies

    What? (the obstacles)

    Where?

    Who? (is going to do it?)

    How? (the message)

Communication Tools

    What could be used?   What will be used?

Evaluation

ADVOCACY FOR SCHOOL LIBRARY PROGRAMS

An effective advocacy plan communicates the role of the school library program by showing how it links to what is important to stakeholders. In this way, stakeholders will become informed advocates for the school library program; also, partnerships with parents, teachers, and administrators can be developed that focus on

- meeting the learning and information needs of students
- making learning and teaching connections
- developing awareness for the importance of information access
- developing an understanding of information literacies and inquiry
- evaluating the effectiveness of the school library program
- increasing the use of school library resources and technologies
- gaining acceptance and support of new and innovative programs

As a result of these efforts, it is possible for opinion leaders in the community to become active supporters and advocates of the school librarian and the school library program. There will be an increased interest and understanding of the program that will result in linking school libraries to other initiatives, interests, and agencies, locally, regionally, and nationally.

To create a successful advocacy plan, the school librarian must be a leader who can employ characteristics of communication, sincerity, decision making, flexibility, and open mindedness. The school librarian must also have a vision for and a willingness to move the plan forward. Promoting the school library program through public relations and marketing is an important part of advocacy. Some of the major activities that can be employed include opinion research, promotions, publicity, and lobbying. The following section provides ideas for public relations, marketing, and advocacy.

The AASL definition for *public relations* involves activities undertaken by organizations to maintain open communication between themselves and their various constituents. Public relations has a place within advocacy. It is a one-way message that tells the library story: "who we are, what we do, and when and where and for whom" (http://www.ala.org/ala/mgrps/divs/aasl/aaslissues/advocacy/definitions.cfm). The messages developed are directed at target audiences.

Examples of public relations activities include the following:

- author visits
- promotional posters
- bookmarks
- scavenger hunts
- story contests
- read-a-thons
- book clubs
- technology fairs

- special story events
- displays

Vehicles used to deliver public relations activities within the school include school e-mail, school Web sites, school library Web sites, announcements, parent newsletters, school newspapers, and social networks. Vehicles to deliver activities outside the school include e-mail, club presentations, local newspapers, radio and television, promotional posters through local businesses, marquees, public service announcements, and press releases.

Marketing, as defined by the AASL advocacy definitions, is a planned and sustained process to assess customers' needs (who they are, what they need, when and where it can be delivered) and then select materials and services to meet those needs (http://www.ala.org/ala/mgrps/divs/aasl/aaslissues/advocacy/definitions.cfm). Marketing usually involves identifying costs. An example of a marketing campaign would be the American Library Association's @ your library® initiative.

On the national level, marketing includes initiatives such as the READ posters by the American Library Association, branding campaigns such as the @ your library campaign and Learning for Life (L4L), and taglines such as "Student Achievement is the Bottom Line" and "Partners for the 21st Century."

Local marketing initiatives might include READ posters, Read a Latte, Bagels and Books, and other planned programs to meet customer needs. Most involve additional costs.

The AASL definition for *advocacy* is an ongoing process of building partnerships so that others will act for and with you, turning passive support into educated action for the school library program (http://www.ala.org/ala/mgrps/divs/aasl/aaslissues/advocacy/definitions.cfm). For the school library program, advocacy involves finding friends and stakeholders of school libraries and creating common agendas and support mechanisms. To be an effective advocate and leader, the school librarian must respect others' needs, perspectives, and priorities. Advocacy involves linking the school library program agenda to the needs of others and building partnerships. Advocacy is ongoing; it is an educational process that raises awareness and benefits the program. It entails speaking up, speaking out, and finding passion and courage while collaborating with and recruiting others to do the same.

Creating an Advocacy Plan

An advocacy plan can be created by using the AASL Advocacy Action Planning Worksheet (http://www.ala.org/ala/mgrps/divs/aasl/aaslissues/toolkits/Advocacy_Action_Plan.doc). Other sources are the American Library Association Web site (http://www.ala.org/) and the AASL home page (http://www.ala.org/ala/mgrps/divs/aasl/aaslissues/issuesadvocacy.cfm) with Advocacy Toolkits.

Through the advocacy planning process, the school librarian must identify the needs of stakeholders and analyze such things as school improvement plans, school mission statements, professional study groups, curriculum initiatives, current literature on best practices, personal contacts, surveys, standard assessment results, and other materials that link to stakeholders' concerns. These efforts will enable the school librarian to make connections with stakeholders by knowing their priorities, speaking their language, involving them, and meeting their needs. In this way, an advocacy plan works toward recruiting others to speak for and with the school librarian in support of the school library program as integral to the educational plan.

EVALUATING SCHOOL LIBRARY PROGRAMS

Evaluation of the School Library Program

The school library program must be evaluated systematically to review overall goals and objectives in relation to instructional needs and to show progress and results. Evaluation provides the basis for decisions regarding the development, continuation, modification, or elimination of policies and procedures. This is a way of examining the efficiency and effectiveness of specific activities and services as they relate to future planning.

Evaluation of the school library program must be an ongoing process. The result of data gathering is twofold: it provides information that can be shared about the program and information that can be used in program planning. The program must achieve the current goals and objectives of the school library program but must also be flexible enough to respond to future needs. Data generated from an evaluation, combined with projections for future needs, can then be translated into a long-term strategic plan that adheres to current guidelines for the school library program.

Procedures for evaluation can range from simple to complex strategies. The more complex procedures produce a great deal of quantitative data but also require a great deal of time to conduct and analyze results. The school librarian needs evaluative data to keep the program on target and communicate success and effective practices while employing a process that is easy to adopt, relatively quick to analyze, and cost effective.

Including Others in the Evaluation Process

Included in this section are materials that require a simple procedure to produce data from seven target populations: legislators, school librarians, parents, administrators, teachers, students, and district or regional directors. The data from these tools can be used to begin program planning and to educate and inform target audiences.

A separate checklist or survey has been developed for each group to determine how much they know about the school library program and their perceptions regarding school library services. It is recommended that all groups be included in the evaluation so that a broad picture can be drawn. An effective school library program depends on the collaborative efforts of all who are responsible for student learning.

Legislators

The checklist for legislators is designed to determine how much they know about school library programs in their states. The checklist can be disseminated at professional association meetings, political meetings, or during lobbying activities. These questions can effectively pique legislators' interests and inspire them to learn more about what is happening in the school library program as well as reveal information about school libraries from their perspective.

Parents

The survey for parents is designed to generate interest in their children's school library program. The checklist can be disseminated at parent-teacher meetings and local service club organization meetings or be made available to library volunteers. In this way, parents can become more inquisitive about the school library program and begin to advocate for excellence.

Administrators, Teachers, and Students

The checklists or surveys for administrators, teachers, and students are designed to measure perceptions held about the school library program within a school. These tools can heighten awareness of the school library program and educate target audiences in addition to being used for gathering data for program improvement or support.

The School Librarians and District and Regional Directors

The checklists and surveys for the school librarians and district/regional supervisors help staff measure how well the program is able to provide the services necessary to achieve excellence.

Also included are checklists related to the school library program covering the roles of the school librarian, priorities for the program, and a program needs assessment.

Evaluation Procedures

Whenever possible, these checklists should be distributed and gathered by the district or regional school library directors. Where no director exists, the school librarian in a district should develop a comprehensive plan to disseminate and collect the checklists.

A concerted effort should be made to form a school library program advisory committee that can interpret and react to the data collected. This group should include the school librarian, district and regional directors, administrators, teachers, and parents. Committee selections require special consideration. Often the school librarian will assume the role as chair. A more powerful strategy may be the naming of a highly influential and credible teacher, parent, or community member to cochair the committee with the school librarian. Outcomes of these efforts may result in an established school improvement and advocacy plan for the school library program.

Making Use of the Checklists and Surveys

These tools can be used in a variety of ways to develop exemplary school library programs for the 21st-century learner. On the basis of the data gathered from the completed checklists and surveys, goals and objectives may be developed. *Empowering Learners: Guidelines for School Library Media Programs* (AASL 2009b) and other published implementation materials can be used to identify the strategies and resources necessary to achieve identified goals. Although not scientific, these checklists and surveys can produce enough data for those involved to make sound decisions regarding the future direction of the local school library program and confirm successful practices. To begin, the school librarian should share data results with the principal. Other possibilities for data use include the following: (1) appointment of a special committee to assess the needs for school library program development, (2) assignment to the standing school library program advisory committee, or (3) participation of the entire faculty.

The process should involve the principal and as many people as possible (e.g., teachers, students, parents, other community members and leaders; the district school library media director; and other district-level administrators).

The rating scales are designed to help assess the current status of the program. When each of the components has been rated, consensus should be reached on one or more priorities for development. An outline of the action plan should list the goals and objectives for implementation with a statement of responsibility and a suggested timeline for completion.

Short-range and long-range plans should be delineated. The number of goals may need to be limited in the beginning to those that can reasonably be accomplished in a brief time. The more difficult goals may require several years for completion.

Plans need to indicate who should be involved at each point in the process, how long the process should take, what components of the program need to be addressed, and the nature of the plans developed through the process, which will vary with each school.

Although the tools have been designed for use at the building level, they may also be used in district, regional, and state planning as well as in library media education programs.

Adapted from *Information Power: Building Partnerships for Learning*, by the American Association of School Librarians, a division of the American Library Association, copyright © 1998, American Library Association. Used with permission.

SCHOOL LIBRARY PROGRAM CHECKLIST: LEGISLATOR FORM

Introduction

If excellence in the school library program is to be achieved, strong partnerships must exist among the state department of education, state legislative bodies, and local school districts. Commitments made by all parties involved will ensure that all students and teachers have equitable access to the services and resources they need to support the teaching-learning process.

The AASL, in its national guidelines *Empowering Learners: Guidelines for School Library Media Programs* (AASL 2009b) and *Standards for the 21st-Century Learner in Action* (AASL 2009a), has identified key elements needed to achieve excellence in school libraries.

This checklist (Table 1.2) has been designed to help school librarians determine whether the state provides the key elements necessary to achieve excellence in school library programs. To use this information effectively,

- investigate the items checked as "Don't Know" to determine whether the item is being provided; these items can then be changed to either "Yes" or "No"

- analyze, then, all items retaining a "No" and establish a priority list for improving school library programs and services; these items can then be considered as the state plans new programs for educational reform

SCHOOL LIBRARY PROGRAM CHECKLIST: SCHOOL LIBRARIAN FORM

Introduction

This checklist (Table 1.3) is intended as a starting point for the school librarian to discover where the school library program stands in relation to *Empowering Learners: Guidelines for School Library Media Programs* (AASL 2009b) and *Standards for the 21st-Century Learner in Action* (AASL 2009a). To use this information effectively,

- checklists should be collected from the teachers and administrators who participated in the evaluation process

- the data should be categorized in order of importance; the advisory committee (consisting of the school librarian, district or regional library directors, administrators, teachers, and parents) should work to develop a realistic long-range plan to address those criteria needed to enhance the services for the school library, and this committee should use planning documents from *Empowering Learners: Guidelines for School Library Media Programs* (AASL 2009b) and *Standards for the 21st-Century Learner in Action* (AASL 2009a) to help guide their efforts

SCHOOL LIBRARY PROGRAM CHECKLIST: PARENT FORM

Introduction

According to *Empowering Learners: Guidelines for School Library Media Programs* (AASL 2009b, 7), the mission of the school library program is to ensure that students and staff are effective users of ideas and information. This mission is accomplished by providing students with both intellectual and physical access to information.

This checklist (Table 1.4) is intended as a starting point for parents to discuss where their children's school library program and the school librarian stand in relation to *Empowering Learners: Guidelines for School Library Media Programs* (AASL 2009b) and *Standards for the 21st-Century Learner in Action* (AASL 2009a). To use this information effectively, take the following steps:

- Those items checked as "Don't Know" should be investigated to determine whether the item is being provided; these items can then be changed to either "Yes" or "No"

- All "No" items remaining should be carefully examined and a priority list should be established; meetings should be scheduled with school administrators, school library media specialists, and teachers so long-range plans can be developed for improving the school library media program in the school

Table 1.2 School Library Program Checklist: Legislator Form

DIRECTIONS: Please read each item carefully. Indicate your knowledge of whether the item is being supported at the state level by checking Yes, No, or Don't Know.

Does the State:	Yes	No	Don't Know
1. Require a certified (credentialed) full-time school librarian in each building?			
2. Provide guidelines based on *Empowering Learners* and *AASL Standards for the 21st-Century Learner* or standards for school library programs?			
3. Identify information literacy skills and the inquiry process within the K–12 curriculum?			
4. Provide state/local funds to assist school libraries in the use of technology as resources and services to students and teachers?			
5. Provide grants for special projects for school library programs?			
6. Encourage schools to seek and use federal, state, and local funds to strengthen the resources of the school library?			
7. Include school libraries in programs funded through federal legislation?			
8. Promote exemplary school library programs at regional, district, and school levels?			
9. Collect data about school library programs and disseminate the findings to the field?			
10. Have qualified full-time staff at the state level who are responsible for providing statewide leadership to school library programs?			
11. Include school libraries in networking activities and interlibrary loan programs so that resources and information can be shared across school, public, and academic boundaries?			
12. Generate publications to assist schools in providing high-quality school library programs and services?			
13. Require the inclusion of school librarians on committees to designate the distribution of federal funds at the local level?			
14. Include school in state funding and sharing of online subscription databases, e-resources, and reference tools?			

Adapted from *Information Power: Building Partnerships for Learning*, by the American Association of School Librarians, a division of the American Library Association, copyright © 1998, American Library Association. Used with permission.

Table 1.3 School Library Program Checklist: School Librarian Form

DIRECTIONS: Please read each item carefully. Rate how well the school library program and the school library media specialist meet each criterion.

Rating Scale
- 0   Nonexistent
- 1   Poor
- 2   Fair
- 3   Good
- 4   Excellent

Please address the following using the rating scale above.

Personnel	0	1	2	3	4
1. One or more certified school librarians are assigned to the building full time.					
2. A district or regional level school library director is available for consultation.					
3. Paid support staff are employed in the school library.					
4. Student assistants work in the school library.					
School Library Instructional Program Partnerships	**0**	**1**	**2**	**3**	**4**
5. A good working relationship exists between the school librarian and the building principal.					
6. The school librarian works collaboratively with faculty and staff in planning, implementing, and assessing instruction that integrates information literacy skills and the inquiry process.					
7. The faculty and staff regularly collaborate with the school librarian for assistance in all phases of instruction.					
8. The school librarian maintains constructive interaction with students in formal and informal settings.					
Information Literacy/Inquiry Program	**0**	**1**	**2**	**3**	**4**
9. Current (within the last five years) information literacy skills and an established the inquiry process are identified within the curriculum and exists in written form.					

Table 1.3 School Library Program Checklist: School Librarian Form (*Continued*)

Information Literacy/Inquiry Program	0	1	2	3	4
10. Teachers and school librarians plan instruction collaboratively to integrate information literacy skills, the inquiry process, and school library resources within the curriculum.					
11. Instruction is assessed collaboratively and meets diverse learning needs.					
12. Students, in groups or individually, may access information through the school library at any time.					
13. The school library has flexible scheduling and access.					
14. The school library climate is conducive to learning					
15. There is commitment to intellectual freedom.					
Facilities	0	1	2	3	4
16. Location of the school library provides easy access, which encourages frequent use.					
17. The school library is an attractive, inviting place.					
18. The design of the school library includes the necessary facilities for comfortable use of materials (recreational reading to electronic access) for students, staff, and school library personnel.					
19. Flexibility in the school library allows varied activities to occur simultaneously.					
20. The school library is available to the school community throughout and beyond the school day.					
Resources and Equipment	0	1	2	3	4
21. The faculty and staff use a wide variety of instructional resources obtained through the school library.					
22. There is a current written board-approved (within the last five years) selection policy.					
23. Information can be obtained via outside sources (such as interlibrary loan and online access).					
24. The school library is automated for circulating and accessing materials.					

Table 1.3 School Library Program Checklist: School Librarian Form (*Continued*)

Resources and Equipment	0	1	2	3	4
25. A written collection development plan exists.					
26. A budget is developed on a yearly basis.					
27. Adequate and ongoing funding is provided for resources and equipment.					
28. Adequate hardware is available to meet access demands.					
29. Online access is reliable and expedient.					
30. Adequate technical support is provided to maintain, upgrade, and troubleshoot hardware, software, and online access demands.					
Professional Development	**0**	**1**	**2**	**3**	**4**
31. The school librarian engages in continuing educational activities.					
32. The school librarian meets with other school librarians in the district to coordinate activities.					
33. The school librarian belongs to state and national professional organizations.					
34. The school librarian reads professional journals on a regular basis.					
35. The school librarian attends workshops and training sessions designed to improve school library services.					
36. The school librarian helps to develop/ implement staff development opportunities related school library resources and services for building level staff.					
37. The school librarian keeps abreast of educational curriculum.					
38. The school librarian keeps abreast of current technology trends.					

Table 1.4 School Library Program Checklist: Parent Form

DIRECTIONS: Please read each item carefully. Indicate whether the item is being provided in the school library by checking Yes, No, or Don't Know.

Does the School Provide	Yes	No	Don't Know
1. A centrally located school library that is available to all students?			
2. A full-time certified school librarian?			
3. Clerical assistance for the operation and management of the school library?			
4. Opportunities for parents to participate in school programs and projects?			
5. A school library that is an interesting and inviting place?			
6. A school librarian who makes students feel welcome in the school library?			
7. A school library with ample space organized to accommodate large groups at one time while still keeping it open for individual students?			
8. A barrier-free learning environment with unimpeded physical access for all users?			
9. A program that stresses the teaching and learning of information literacy skills and an inquiry process across the curriculum?			
10. Student assignments that require use of the school library?			
11. School library resources and services, including those that take advantage of various technologies and satisfy the needs of the entire school population?			
12. Opportunities for the school librarian and teachers to collaborate to plan instruction?			
13. Resources that are adequate in kind and number to support the curriculum as well as individualized and instructional needs?			
14. Encouragement for students to use resources beyond those provided by the school library?			
15. A school library budget that supports the program in quantitative terms?			
16. Opportunities for the programs and services of the school library to be communicated?			
17. An up-to-date, well-balanced collection of resources, including print, nonprint, digital, and online?			
18. Adequate hardware to meet access demands?			
19. Online access that is reliable and expedient?			

SCHOOL LIBRARY PROGRAM CHECKLIST: ADMINISTRATOR FORM

Introduction

According to *Empowering Learners: Guidelines for School Library Media Programs* (AASL 2009b), the mission of the school library program is to ensure that students and staff are effective users of ideas and information. This mission is accomplished by providing students with intellectual and physical access to information.

This checklist (Table 1.5) is intended to be a starting point for the administrator to discover where the school library program stands in relation to *Empowering Learners: Guidelines for School Library Media Programs* (AASL 2009b). It is recommended that administrators become familiar with the guidelines before responding to this form. To use this form effectively, the following steps should be taken:

- Each item should be read carefully.

- Ratings should be established showing how well the school library meets each criterion.

- The checklist should be returned to the school librarian. Responses will be taken into account when meetings are held with the library staff, teachers, and parents in a partnership effort to develop a long-range plan to improve the school library program.

SCHOOL LIBRARY PROGRAM CHECKLIST: TEACHER FORM

Introduction

According to *Empowering Learners: Guidelines for School Library Media Programs* (AASL 2009b), the mission of the school library program is to ensure that students and staff are effective users of ideas and information. This mission is accomplished by providing students with both intellectual and physical access to information.

This checklist (Table 1.6) is intended as a starting point for the teacher to discover where the school library program stands in relation to *Empowering Learners: Guidelines for School Library Media Programs* (AASL 2009b).

SCHOOL LIBRARY PROGRAM CHECKLIST: STUDENT FORM

Introduction

The education of students is the major rationale for the existence of school library programs in today's schools. If this reasoning is valid, students must be given the opportunity to state their points of view. Student opinion is a major indicator of program success. It is anticipated that use of the student questionnaire by school library personnel will indicate changes of direction with respect to the learning environment.

The student questionnaire is in two parts. Part A (Table 1.7A) is general in nature. Part B (Table 1.7B) may be used to gather more specific data.

Table 1.5 Assessing the School Library Program: Administrator Form

DIRECTIONS: Read each item carefully. Rate how well the school library program and assigned personnel meet each criterion. Return the checklist to your school librarian. Responses will be discussed at a partnership meeting with the library staff, teachers, students, and parents in a collaborative effort to develop a long-range plan to improve the school library program.

Rating Scale
  0 **Not at all, and no planning under way**
  1 **Not at all, but planning under way**
  2 **Partially**
  3 **Mostly**
  4 **Totally**

Personnel	0	1	2	3	4
1. There is at least one certified school librarian assigned to the building at one time.					
2. A district- or regional-level school library director is available for consultation.					
3. There is at least one paid support staff member employed at the school library.					
4. Student assistants work in the school library.					
5. The school library is an inviting and attractive place.					
6. The facilities are adequate for the school library needs as well as for technology use.					
7. Flexibility in the school library allows varied activities to occur simultaneously.					
8. No physical barriers exist at the school library.					
9. The school library is available to the school community throughout and beyond the school day and the online resources are available 24–7.					
Resources and Equipment	0	1	2	3	4
10. The faculty uses a wide range of instructional resources, which they obtain through the school library.					
11. There is a current (within the last five years) board-approved selection policy for materials acquired for the school library.					
12. Information can be obtained virtually 24–7 from the school library.					
13. Management functions of the school library are automated.					
14. A written collection development plan exists.					
15. A budget is developed yearly.					
16. Adequate and ongoing funding is provided for resources and equipment.					

Table 1.5 Assessing the School Library Program: Administrator Form (*Continued*)

Resources and Equipment	0	1	2	3	4
17. Adequate hardware and technology is available to meet access and resource demands.					
18. Online access is reliable and expedient.					
19. Adequate technical support is provided to maintain, upgrade, and troubleshoot hardware, software, and online access demands.					
Program	**0**	**1**	**2**	**3**	**4**
20. The faculty regularly collaborates with the school librarian for assistance in the planning and implementation of research/ project-based assignments using inquiry-based learning.					
21. The school librarian has developed an instructional program partnership with faculty, staff, and parents and works closely with them in planning, implementing, and assessing instruction.					
22. A current list (within the past five years) of information and multiple literacy skills is identified from the curriculum.					
23. The delivery of information literacy skills is integrated into and correlated with classroom instruction through collaborative planning among teachers and the school librarian.					
24. The school library operates on a flexible schedule.					
25. The library climate is conducive to learning.					
Professional Development	**0**	**1**	**2**	**3**	**4**
26. The school librarian is a member of a school library professional organization.					
27. The school librarian engages in library as well as other continuing education activities.					
28. The school district librarians meet as a group to coordinate activities.					
29. Funding is available for continuing professional education activities for the school library staff.					
30. The school librarian helps plan/implement professional development activities for staff related to school library resources and services.					

Table 1.6 Assessing the School Library Program: Teacher Form

DIRECTIONS: Read each item carefully. Rate how well the school library program meets each criterion. Return the checklist to your school librarian. Responses will be discussed at a partnership meeting with the library staff, teachers, students, and parents in a collaborative effort to develop a long-range plan to improve the school library program.

Rating Scale
- **DK** **Don't know**
- **0** **Not at all, and no planning under way**
- **1** **Not at all, but planning under way**
- **2** **Partially**
- **3** **Mostly**
- **4** **Totally**

Personnel	DK	0	1	2	3	4
1. There is at least one certified librarian assigned to the building at one time.						
2. There is at least one paid support staff member employed at the school library.						
3. Student and adult volunteers assist in the school library.						
Facilities	DK	0	1	2	3	4
4. The school library is an inviting and attractive place.						
5. The facilities are adequate for the school library needs as well as for technology.						
6. Space and flexible arrangement in the school library allow varied activities to occur simultaneously.						
7. All students have physical access to the school library in the school environment and virtually 24–7.						
8. The location of the school library permits students easy access to the collection.						
Resources and Equipment	DK	0	1	2	3	4
9. The faculty uses a wide range of instructional resources, which they obtain through the school library.						
10. There is a current (within the last five years) board-approved selection policy for materials acquired by the school library.						
11. Information can be obtained virtually 24–7 from the school library.						
12. Adequate funding is available for the purchase of print and digital resources, equipment, and technologies.						
13. Technical support is provided to maintain, upgrade, and troubleshoot hardware, software, and online access demands.						
14. Online access is 24–7 and is reliable and expedient.						
15. Adequate technology is available to meet demands.						

Table 1.6 Assessing the School Library Program: Teacher Form (*Continued*)

Program	DK	0	1	2	3	4
16. The faculty regularly collaborates with the school librarian for assistance in the planning and implementation of research/ project-based assignments using inquiry-based learning.						
17. The school librarian has developed an instructional program partnership with faculty, staff, and parents and works closely with them in planning, implementing, and evaluating instruction.						
18. Teachers meet regularly with the school librarian for implementing and assessing instruction and for incorporating information literacy skills and school library resources.						
19. The school library program is evaluated regularly.						
20. Information and multiple literacy skills have been identified within the curriculum.						
21. The delivery of information literacy skills is integrated into and correlated with classroom instruction across the curriculum.						
22. Students may access information through the school library program throughout and beyond the school day.						
23. Digital and print information and resources can be obtained from outside sources.						

Adapted from *Information Power: Building Partnerships for Learning,* by the American Association of School Librarians, a division of the American Library Association, copyright © 1998, American Library Association. Used with permission.

Table 1.7A Assessing the School Library Program: Student Form Part A—General

DIRECTIONS: Read each item carefully. Indicate how well the school library program meets the following criteria. Please answer the questions using the rating scale below.

Rating Scale
  Yes
  Sometimes
  No

	Yes	Some-times	No
1. Are students given times to access school library resources for assignments?			
2. Are students allowed to go to the school library whenever there is free time?			
3. Does the school library sometimes get so crowded that it is impossible to get in?			
4. Do students get help in the school library when needed?			
5. Do classes go to the school library regularly to learn information literacy skills?			
6. Does the school library usually have the materials needed for assignments?			
7. Are students taught how to find materials in the school library and from online databases?			
8. Has the school librarian asked input from students in choosing the resources for the school library?			
9. Does the school allow students to take home materials and/or equipment from the school library?			
10. Does the school library provide computers, printers, digital cameras, and other technologies to aid in the completion of homework?			
11. Do students get help creating project/research based assignments from the school librarian?			
12. Does using the school library resources makes classes more interesting?			
13. Do students know when new books, online databases, computer applications, or materials are available in the school library?			
14. Do students at your school like to go to the school library?			
15. Have students in the school been taught the skills necessary to be good consumers of information?			
16. Are students aware of online/networked resources available through the school library program?			
17. Is the school library automated for circulation and collection searching?			
Comments:			

Table 1.7B Assessing the School Library Program: Student Form Part B—Specific Data

DIRECTIONS: Read each item carefully. Indicate how well the school library program meets the following criteria. Please answer the questions using the rating scale below.

Rating Scale
   Yes
   Sometimes
   No

	Yes	Some-times	No
1. Is the school library available to students whenever their schedule permits time to go there?			
2. Are classes ever scheduled at fixed times in the school library?			
3. Are the school library facilities too crowded?			
4. Are the school library facilities too noisy?			
5. Are the school library facilities too limited?			
6. Is learning easier and more interesting for students in classes where a variety of technology is used?			
7. Are teachers trying something new or different concerning the use of information, materials, equipment, and technology?			
8. Does it ever happen that students cannot obtain all the materials or resources they need from the school library?			
9. Does the school librarian teach students how to find print and digital materials for assignments?			
10. Does school policy allow students access to equipment and technologies to help with assignments in the school library?			
11. Does school policy allow students to take home materials (other than books) from the school library?			
12. Do students use the school library frequently throughout the year to check out materials/resources?			
13. Do students have access to online resources at school and at home?			
14. Are students ever been asked to help select materials for the school library?			
15. If a student were to suggest a book or other material for purchase for the school library, would his or her suggestion be seriously considered?			
16. Are students permitted to use school equipment and technologies to produce presentations, pod casts, movies, and other projects?			
17. Is there a school librarian or other school personnel in the school library to help students produce presentations, pod casts, movies, and other projects?			
18. Are digital projectors, cameras, and other technologies available to check out at the school library?			

Table 1.7B Assessing the School Library Program: Student Form
     Part B—Specific Data (*Continued*)

	Yes	Some-times	No
19. During the past year, has any teacher helped you obtain specific materials for your use?			
20. Do students know when new books or materials are available in the school library?			
21. Do teachers encourage students to individually use print materials?			
22. Do teachers encourage students to individually use visual materials?			
23. Do teachers encourage students to individually use open source technologies (e.g., blogs, wikis, nings, Moodles)?			
24. Do teachers encourage students to individually use online information?			
25. Do teachers encourage students to individually use new computer software applications?			
26. Are digital resources used as part of classroom instruction?			
27. Do students like to go to the school library?			
28. Does the school library provide adequate computers and technology for student use?			
29. Are students instructed on information literacy, how to locate online resources, and to be a good consumer of information?			
Comments:			

SCHOOL LIBRARY PROGRAM CHECKLIST: DISTRICT AND REGIONAL DIRECTOR FORM

Introduction

The district, regional, and state school library leaders should work in partnership with the school librarian, principals, curriculum specialists, and administrators.

This series of checklists (Tables 1.8–1.11) are (Table 1.5) is intended to be a starting point for the school library district or regional directors and state leaders to discover where their programs and leadership stand in relation to *Empowering Learners: Guidelines for School Library Media Programs* (AASL 2009b) and *Standards for the 21st-Century Learner* (AASL 2009a). To use this information effectively, the following steps should be taken:

- Checklists completed by the school librarian, administrators, teachers, parents, and legislators should be collected.

- A meeting of school librarians, teachers, administrators, district and regional directors, and parents should be arranged.

- Those items that need to be addressed to achieve excellence in the school library should be categorized in order of importance.

- A realistic, long-range plan should be developed using planning documents related to *Empowering Learners: Guidelines for School Library Media Programs* (AASL 2009b) and *Standards for the 21st-Century Learner in Action* (AASL 2009a).

Table 1.8 School Library Program Checklist: District and Regional Director Form

DIRECTIONS: Read each item carefully. Rate how well the following support is provided for the items listed. Responses will be discussed at a partnership meeting with the library staff, teachers, students, and parents in a collaborative effort to develop a long-range plan to improve the school library program.

Rating Scale
0   Not at all, and no planning under way
1   Not at all, but planning under way
2   Partially
3   Mostly
4   Totally

Please answer the following questions using the rating scale above. As a director, do you:

Leadership	0	1			4
1. Advise in the use of technologies and provide for demonstrations?					
2. Provide guidance in program planning and curriculum writing?					

Table 1.8 School Library Program Checklist: District and Regional Director Form (*Continued*)

Leadership	0	1	2	3	4
3. Coordinate staff development programs for school librarians, faculty, support staff, parents, school board, administrators, and community members?					
4. Interpret school library standards, requirements, laws, and policies?					
5. Serve as liaison with other supervisors and administrators?					
6. Participate in local, state, and national library professional organizations?					
7. Assist planning committees and architects in remodeling existing facilities and designing new facilities?					
Communication	0	1	2	3	4
8. Serve as an advocate for school libraries with teachers, administrators, board members, parents, and community?					
9. Share current information on research, technology, and instructional strategies with school librarians, principals, and other district administrators?					
10. Provide school library orientation to teachers, administrators, and support staff?					
11. Report the impact of the school library program to school groups and the public?					
12. Initiate and participate in professional public relations activities?					
13. Conduct local research relative to school library services and the impact on student learning and publicize results?					
14. Have a school library support group consisting of school librarians, teachers, administrators, and parents to make recommendations to improve the services of the school library?					
15. Identify, with other instructional leaders, research and information literacy skills within the curriculum?					
16. Serve on instructional, curriculum, textbook, and new program adoption committees?					
17. Design and implement K–12 school library program integration with the total educational plan?					
18. Coordinate the development and use of specialized collections?					
19. Compile and update a list of curriculum-based information literacy skills for use within the district?					
Administration	0	1	2	3	4
...chool library budget?					
...ry personnel?					
...ing					

Table 1.8 School Library Program Checklist: District and Regional Director Form (*Continued*)

Administration	0	1	2	3	4
23. Compile, maintain, and report statistical data regarding services and collections?					
24. Coordinate or provide technical services for processing materials and equipment?					
25. Evaluate the impact of the school library program on the instructional program at the district and school levels?					
26. Monitor the status of district compliance with regard to regional, state, and national accreditation requirements?					
27. Identify sources of funding and write proposals for grants?					
28. Participate in the legislative process to encourage financial support for school library programs?					

Adapted from *Information Power: Building Partnerships for Learning*, by the American Association of School Librarians, a division of the American Library Association, copyright © 1998, American Library Association. Used with permission.

Table 1.9 School Library Program Checklist: District Leadership Form

DIRECTIONS: Read each item carefully. Rate how well the district school library director performs the principle functions. Return the checklist to your school librarian. Responses will be discussed at a partnership meeting with the library staff, teachers, students, and parents in a collaborative effort to develop a long-range plan to improve the school library program.

Rating Scale
  0   Nonexistent
  1   Poor
  2   Fair
  3   Good
  4   Excellent

Please address the following using the rating scale above.

Leadership	0	1	2	3	4
1. Develops an effective plan and process for providing school library programs that support the mission, goals, and objectives of the school district					
2. Provides leadership and guidance to the school library staff in program planning, curriculum development, budgeting, in-service activities, facility use, media production, and use of technology					
3. Participates in curriculum development, facility planning, personnel staff, budget and management committees, and task forces and teams at the administrative level					
4. Articulates a code of ethics that promotes adherence to copyright laws					
5. Advocates the principles of intellectual freedom that govern the universal right to read and access information and ideas					
6. Encourages the use of new technologies to support teaching and learning					
7. Directs the district's participation in school library networking					
8. Serves as liaison with supervisory and administrative personnel at local, state, and national levels					
9. Fosters the development of exemplary library programs at each educational level and assists the programs in meeting regional, state, national, and professional standards					
10. Provides district in-service programs for school librarians to foster leadership, competence, and creativity in developing programs					
11. Assists principals, school librarians, and others in applying district policies that relate to library programs					

Table 1.9 School Library Program Checklist: District Leadership Form (*Continued*)

Leadership	0	1	2	3	4
12. Participates actively in state and national professional associations and encourages a high level of participation by other district school library personnel and building-level personnel					
Consultation	**0**	**1**	**2**	**3**	**4**
13. Assists school librarians in developing program goals and objectives					
14. Promotes expression of programs that integrate the teaching of skills for finding, evaluating, and using information with the teaching of subject content					
15. Demonstrates methods for effective integration of school library activities and instructional units in building-level programs					
16. Consults with planning committees and architects when new or remodeled facilities are designed					
Communication	**0**	**1**	**2**	**3**	**4**
17. Advises district and school administrators of new developments in school library programs, technology, instructional strategies, and research					
18. Conducts orientation meetings on the school library program for teachers, administrators, and support staff					
19. Provides building-level school librarians with information regarding computer-based applications for circulation procedures and public access catalogs					
20. Develops and implements plans for presenting and publicizing school library programs and services					
21. Prepares reports for district and school administrators on the impact of building-level programs on the instructional process					
22. Submits reports to the local board of education, to state and national agencies, to the library staff, and to the public					
Coordination	**0**	**1**	**2**	**3**	**4**
23. Identifies, in coordination with district and building-level instructional leaders, the information skills inherent within the curriculum areas					
24. Participates in curriculum development and implementation through membership on instructional curriculum, textbook, and new program adoption committees					
25. Coordinates the planning and development of K–12 library programs that serve the students and staff within the school					
26. Coordinates the acquisition and circulation of specialized collections that enrich the curriculum for all grade levels					

Table 1.9 School Library Program Checklist: District Leadership Form (*Continued*)

Administration	0	1	2	3	4
27. Works with the principal in selecting and evaluating school library personnel					
28. Works with the principal to ensure that the school library program furthers the instructional process					
29. Assists school librarians and principals in developing building-level school library budgets					
30. Develops the district school library budget, including any allocation for each school, in cooperation with the building principals and school librarians					
31. Interprets the library program and associated budgets for the appropriate administrators					
32. Furnishes a wide range of resources and services to the school library program and classroom, for example, video library, production services, television studio, printing service, computer-assisted instruction, telecommunications, automated systems, and loan of expensive or infrequently used materials or equipment					
33. Distributes preview and on-approval materials for evaluation/purchase					
34. Monitors state and federal laws pertaining the school library programs					
35. Monitors the adequacy of collections and equipment to provide data on relevance and currency					
36. Arranges for building-level school librarians to evaluate new resources and electronic equipment					
37. Negotiates contracts and supervises purchase and installation of all resources					
38. Manages technical services for acquiring and processing resources and for maintaining and circulation of district-owned materials and equipment					
39. Encourages teachers, administrators, and parents to visit library programs within and outside the district					
40. Monitors and publicizes the status of district compliance with regional, state, and national accreditation requirements and school library standards					
41. Provides a professional library collection as well as media and information services for educators					
42. Seeks and administers grants from federal, state, and regional agencies and from foundations					
43. Evaluates the impact of school library programs at the district and school levels					

Table 1.9 School Library Program Checklist: District Leadership Form

Priorities for district leadership are:

1. _____

   _____

2. _____

   _____

3. _____

   _____

Adapted from *Information Power: Building Partnerships for Learning,* by the American Association of School Librarians, a division of the American Library Association, copyright © 1998, American Library Association. Used with permission.

Table 1.10 School Library Program Checklist: Regional Leadership Form

DIRECTIONS: Read each item carefully. Rate how well school library regional leadership performs the principle functions. Return the checklist to your designated person.

Rating Scale
- 0 Nonexistent
- 1 Poor
- 2 Fair
- 3 Good
- 4 Excellent

Many services provided by regional school library programs are similar to those provided by district-level school library programs; therefore only those not commonly provided at other levels are listed below.

Please address the following using the rating scale above.

Leadership	0	1	2	3	4
1. Offers staff development programs for school librarians, teachers, and administrators					
2. Provides leadership in evaluating the impact of new and existing technologies and program features					
3. Promotes the adoption of new and tested technologies in the region; sets up pilot programs to test new technologies					
4. Plans for the installation of telecommunication services such as distance learning and teleconferencing					
5. Participates actively in state and national professional associations and encourages a high level of participation by district and school library personnel					
Consultation	0	1	2	3	4
6. Recommends and encourages visits to exemplary school library programs					
7. Assists school libraries in public relations/advocacy activities					
Communication	0	1	2	3	4
8. Develops publications, newsletters, videos, and other types of communication sources for dissemination to the schools					
9. Alerts schools to legislative initiatives that pertain to or affect school library programs, curriculum change, graduation requirements, or other matters of interest to educators					
Coordination	0	1	2	3	4
10. Coordinates school library program participation in multitype networks					

Table 1.10 School Library Program Checklist: Regional Leadership Form (*Continued*)

	0	1	2	3	4
11. Coordinates cooperative preview and purchasing of school library resources and equipment, cooperative bidding, state contracts, and licensing agreements					
Administration	**0**	**1**	**2**	**3**	**4**
12. Produces or distributes instructional television programs, specialized video, or other media					
13. Furnishes technical processing services and access to national bibliographic utilities					
14. Negotiates rights for distribution, purchase, and rental/lease of media resources to save money through cooperative acquisition and to ensure legal compliance with copyright considerations					
15. Establishes a preview and examination center for instructional materials and the emerging technologies					
16. Establishes an oversees networking system for member schools, including resource sharing, databases, telecommunications, cooperative collection development agreements, cooperative staff, and curriculum development					
17. Makes available computer and database for administration and instruction					
18. Develops specialized collections as appropriate					
19. Provides and arranges maintenance of audiovisual and computer equipment owned by member schools					
20. Provides printing services, delivery services, media production, and distribution service					

Priorities for regional leadership are:

1. _____

_____

2. _____

_____

3. _____

_____

Table 1.11 School Library Program Checklist: State Leadership Form

Rating Scale
  0 Nonexistent
  1 Poor
  2 Fair
  3 Good
  4 Excellent

Please address the following using the rating scale above.

Leadership	0	1	2	3	4
1. Promotes exemplary professional practices and programs at regional, district, and school levels					
2. Participates in developing state standards and/or guidelines for school library programs and criteria for certification of school library personnel					
3. Develops plans for state-based research on school library programs and seeks funding for such research					
4. Seeks legislative initiatives in support of school library programs					
5. Ensures that state mandates concerning school library programs are met					
6. Clarifies accreditation issues, including evaluation of school library programs and school library education programs, and participates in curricular development of these programs					
7. Participates actively in state and national professional associations and encourages a high level of participation by district, regional, and school library personnel					
Consultation	**0**	**1**	**2**	**3**	**4**
8. Provides staff development programs on philosophy, concepts, and trends of school library programs to administrators, supervisors, school librarians, curriculum directors, and teachers					
9. Offers consultative services to districts concerning new technologies and services and the planning of school library facilities					
10. Guides districts and regions in the implementation of state policies, laws, and regulations					
11. Assists schools, districts, and regions in dealing with such problems as censorship challenges					
12. Participates in the development of state curricular materials and correlates them with school library services and information literacy skills					

Table 1.11 School Library Program Checklist: State Leadership Form (*Continued*)

Consultation	0	1	2	3	4
13. Reviews school library education programs for accredited program status					

Communication	0	1	2	3	4
14. Collects data and disseminates information on school library programs in the state					
15. Promotes school library programs through public relations activities					
16. Receives and disseminates information from state and federal reports related to school library programs					
17. Generates publications to assist district- and building-level personnel in providing improved services					

Coordination	0	1	2	3	4
18. Encourages the use of interlibrary loan and cooperative agreements among school, public, academic, and other libraries					
19. Works cooperatively with state school library associations and other state educational service agencies, for example, the state department of education and Educational Service Units					

Administration	0	1	2	3	4
20. Interprets and adopts the policies of the state board of education as well as state and federal laws and regulations relating to school libraries in the educational program					
21. Evaluates school library programs in schools or districts and makes recommendations for their improvement					
22. Supervises the development of long-range plans for effective school library programs					
23. Makes budget recommendations based on needs assessment for consideration by the appropriate state agency					
24. Develops guidelines for administration of federal and state funds					
25. Performs a clearinghouse function for information about state school library services					
26. Plans state television programs, services, and networks where appropriate					

Table 1.11 School Library Program Checklist: State Leadership Form (*Continued*)

Priorities for state leadership are:

1. _____

   _____

2. _____

   _____

3. _____

   _____

SCHOOL LIBRARY PROGRAM ASSESSMENT

Introduction

In order to make ongoing plans for improvement of the school library program, steps for program assessment must be undertaken. The following series of checklists and surveys (Tables 1.12–1.14) are intended to assess school library programs, the priorities and the needs of the school library program. To use this information effectively, the following steps should be taken:

- Checklists completed by the school librarian, administrators, teachers, parents, or students should be collected by a designated person.

- A meeting of school librarians, teachers, administrators, district and regional directors, and parents should be arranged.

- Those items that need to be addressed to achieve leadership excellence for school libraries should be categorized in order of importance.

Table 1.12 Checklist for School Library Programs

DIRECTIONS: Read each item carefully and address each using the rating scale below.

Rating Scale
- 0   Nonexistent
- 1   Poor
- 2   Fair
- 3   Good
- 4   Excellent

Program	0	1	2	3	4
1. The school library program plays a critical role in teaching/ learning activities.					
2. The school library program is fully integrated into the curriculum and serves the schools educational goals and objectives by providing access to information and ideas for the entire school community.					
3. Information literacy skills are identified and integrated and taught throughout the curriculum.					
4. The principal, the school librarian, teachers, and students work together to ensure that the program contributes fully to the educational process in the school.					
5. The school library program offers such traditional resources and technologies as teaching and learning tools.					

(Continued)

Table 1.12 Checklist for School Library Programs (*Continued*)

Program	0	1	2	3	4
6. The program is housed in a school library that provides adequate and appropriate space for all the resources and activities of the program.					
7. The school library is convenient, comfortable, and aesthetically inviting.					

Priorities for development of the school library program are:

1. _____

2. _____

3. _____

_____

The School Librarian's Roles and Responsibilities

Rating Scale
   0   Nonexistent
   1   Poor
   2   Fair
   3   Good
   4   Excellent

Teacher	0	1	2	3	4
1. Through collaborative efforts of teachers and school librarians, information literacy skills are taught as an integral part of the content and objectives of the schools curriculum.					
2. Information literacy includes instruction in accessing, evaluating, and communicating information and in the production of media.					
3. The school librarian collaborates effectively with teachers to plan, teach, and evaluate instruction in information access, use, and communication skills.					
4. Assistance is provided in the use of technology to access information in and outside the school library.					
5. Teachers and other adults are offered learning opportunities related to new technologies, use, and production of a variety of media and laws and policies regarding information.					
6. The school librarian uses a variety of instructional methods with different user groups and demonstrate the effective use of newer media and technologies.					

Table 1.12 Checklist for School Library Programs (*Continued*)

Teacher	0	1	2	3	4
7. The school librarian is knowledgeable about current research on effective teaching and learning.					
8. The school librarian is capable of assessing teaching and learning information needs.					

Priorities for development of the school librarian's roles and responsibilities are:

1. _____

2. _____

3. _____

_____

Information Specialist	0	1	2	3	4
9. The school librarian makes resources available to students and teachers through a systematically developed collection within the school and through access to resources outside the school.					
10. Access to the school library collection is provided by an accurate and efficient retrieval system that uses the expanding searching capabilities of the computer.					
11. Students receive assistance in identifying, locating, and interpreting information housed inside and outside the school library.					
12. Students and teachers have access to the school library and to qualified professional staff throughout the school day. Class visits are scheduled flexibly to encourage use at point of need.					
13. Policies and procedures ensure that access to information is not impeded by fees, loan restrictions, or online searching charges.					
14. Teachers, students, parents, and administrators are informed of new materials, equipment, and services that meet their information needs.					
15. Students at remote sites are provided with access to information.					

(Continued)

Table 1.12 Checklist for School Library Programs (*Continued*)

Priorities for development of the school librarian's roles and responsibilities are:

1. _____

2. _____

3. _____

_____

Instructional Partner	0	1	2	3	4
16. School librarians participate in building-, district-, department-, and grade-level curriculum development and assessment projects on a regular basis.					
17. School librarians collaborate with teachers in using information resources, acquiring and assessing instructional materials, and incorporating information literacy skills into the classroom curriculum.					
18. School librarians use a systematic instructional development process in working with teachers to improve the integration of information literacy skills into the classroom curriculum.					
19. School librarians provide leadership in the assessment, evaluation, and adoption of information and instructional technologies.					

Priorities for development of the school librarian's roles and responsibilities are:

1. _____

2. _____

3. _____

_____

Program Administrator	0	1	2	3	4
20. The mission, goals, and objectives of the school library program are clearly understood and fully supported by the administrative and educational staff, the students, and the community.					
21. Responsibility for leading and managing the school library program is a collaborative effort led by the school librarian to develop library goals, establish priorities, and allocate the resources necessary to accomplish the mission.					

Table 1.12 Checklist for School Library Programs (*Continued*)

Program Administrator	0	1	2	3	4
22. The school librarian involves school and district school library program administrators, the school library staff, school administrators, teachers, students, and community members, as appropriate, in the program planning process.					
23. As part of the planning process, the school library program is evaluated on a regular basis to review overall goals and objectives in relation to user and instructional needs and to assess the efficiency and effectiveness of specific activities.					
24. Program and personnel evaluations follow district-wide policies and procedures, focus on performance, and are based on appropriately collected data.					
25. The planning process results in periodic reports that emphasize and document progress toward stated goals and objectives.					
26. The school librarian works with others to cooperatively plan the school library budget.					
27. Through budget development, the school librarian seeks sufficient funds to provide for the resources and personnel necessary to achieve the goals and objectives of the school library program.					
28. The school librarian advocates for adequate support staff fundamental to the implementation of effective school library programs at the school and district levels. The quality and size of the professional and support staff are directly related to the range and level of services provided.					
29. The school librarian oversees training, support, and evaluation of the school library staff in their roles that are key to the success of the program.					
30. The school librarian demonstrates the importance of the school library programs in education, publicizes available services and resources to students and staff, serves on school and district-wide committees, and participates in community-wide projects.					
Leader	0	1	2	3	4
31. The mission, goals, and objectives of the school library program are linked to stakeholder goals and issues.					
32. The school librarian leads the effort, involving others, to create and implement a long-term school library advocacy plan.					

(Continued)

Table 1.12 Checklist for School Library Programs (*Continued*)

Leader	0	1	2	3	4
33. The school librarian ensures that school library mission, goals, and priorities are reflected in the advocacy plan.					
34. The school librarian takes initiative to provide periodic reports that emphasize and document progress toward stated goals and objectives of the advocacy plan.					
35. The school librarian advocates for the school library by serving on school and district-wide committees and participates in community-wide projects.					
36. The school librarian uses various tools to communicate with stakeholders (e.g., Web sites, newsletters, e-mail, blogs, presentations).					

Priorities for leadership are:

1. _____

2. _____

3. _____

_____

Table 1.13 Priorities of School Library Programs

Your Assignment: Level:

_____ School Librarian   _____ Elementary

_____ Teacher   _____ Middle School/Junior High

_____ Administrator   _____ Senior High

Directions

Indicate your opinion of the importance of the following services provided by the school library staff
by circling the appropriate number.

Rating Scale
1. **Not Important**
2. **Somewhat Important**
3. **Very Important**
DK **Don't Know**

School Library Staff in Our School	1	2	3	DK
1. Preview, evaluate, select, and acquire school library materials and equipment in cooperation with others in the learning community.				
2. Analyze instructional resource needs for the school library and plan an appropriate budget.				
3. Reevaluate materials in relation to changing curriculum content, new instructional methods, and needs of students and staff.				
4. Organize and maintain the catalog.				
5. Plan and implement an efficient system that circulates school library materials				
6. Maintain, upgrade, and expand equipment resources to meet changing needs of staff and students.				
7. Plan and execute promotional school library programs (e.g., Book Week) for students and staff.				
8. Provide school library materials that reflect a diversity of ideas, experiences, and cultural perspectives.				
9. Analyze and support curriculum in all subject areas.				
10. Provide guidance to students and staff in the use of reference materials.				
11. Collaborate with others to identify, integrate, and teach information literacy skills and use of resources within the curriculum.				
12. Collaborate with teachers to help students master a research process.				

(Continued)

Table 1.13 Priorities of School Library Programs (*Continued*)

School Library Staff in Our School	1	2	3	DK
13. Encourage students to read by making materials available that reflect a wide variety of reading and interest levels.				
14. Encourage exploration, discrimination, and enjoyment of literature and reading.				
15. Conduct in-services related to school library resources, services, and technology.				
16. Maintain contact with other school librarians to promote the enhancement of knowledge and skills.				
17. Promote lifelong learning skills by teaching students the value of school library resources.				
18. Create an organized and accessible facility containing resources that allow students and staff to easily locate needed materials and equipment for their use.				
19. Provide assistance in identifying, communicating, and interpreting information and learning needs.				
20. Serve as a liaison between the school, central office, and community to enhance services and resources for students and staff.				
21. Provide users with materials, equipment, and facilities for production functions adhering to copyright guidelines.				
22. Provide instructional television service, including off-air and live taping, scheduling, and maintaining equipment.				
23. Promote intellectual freedom and equitable access to information.				
School Library Programs Should Have	**1**	**2**	**3**	**DK**
24. An online system for circulating school library resources.				
25. A catalog that uses expanded searching capabilities to provide access to resources within the school library.				
26. Use of appropriate technology (e.g., electronic encyclopedias and atlases) to provide access to information sources in the school library.				
27. Use of appropriate technology (e.g., e-mail and online databases) to provide access to information sources outside the school library.				
28. Adequate technical support for the operation, updating, and maintenance of software and hardware.				

Adapted from assessment tools developed by ESU #18 Evaluation Team for the Lincoln Public Schools Library Media Services Department.

Table 1.14 School Library Program Needs Assessment

Your Assignment: Level:

_____ School Librarian   _____ Elementary

_____ Teacher   _____ Middle School/Junior High

_____ Administrator   _____ Senior High

Directions: Write the number from the scale below that describes to what extent you think each of the following statements is characteristic of your school library and then write in the number that describes how you think it should be. If you cannot make a judgment, write DK (Don't Know).

Scale: 1   2   3   4   5   6   7   DK

       NOT AT ALL   TO A GREAT   I DON'T
                                  EXTENT   KNOW

Part A: The SLMP in Our School	What Is	What Should Be
1. The climate in the school library is conducive to use by students and staff.		
2. The school library staff exhibits a service-oriented attitude.		
3. The schedules of school library staff are flexible enough to permit interruption and respond to user needs.		
4. The school library is available to more than one group at the same time, making possible prescheduled use and spur-of-the-moment use.		
5. Budget is sufficient to support regularly scheduled replacement of worn and outdated school library materials.		
6. The budget provides for annual acquisition of new materials to support curricular needs.		
7. The school library collection includes instructional resources selected to meet the needs of all students.		
8. Sufficient funding is available to support online fees and telephone costs for expedient and reliable electronic information services.		
9. Sufficient funding is available to support acquisition, maintenance, and upgrading of technology that provides access to electronic information services inside and outside the school library.		
Part B: Promoting Student Learning through the Use of School Library Resources Student in Our School	**What Is**	**What Should Be**
1. Learn reference skills well enough to feel confident in using a variety of tools (e.g., online catalog, atlas, encyclopedia, online databases, digital media)		

(Continued)

Table 1.14 School Library Program Needs Assessment (*Continued*)

Part B: Promoting Student Learning through the Use of School Library Resources Student in Our School	What Is	What Should Be
2. Apply reference skills in a variety of situations (e.g., completing assignments by using city library resources)		
3. Learn to use school library equipment (e.g., digital cameras, data projectors, computers)		
4. Participate in activities that promote individual reading enjoyment and encourage personal reading		
5. Develop an awareness of and appreciation for literature		
6. Use a variety of information sources from the school relevant to classroom assignments and personal needs		
7. Use the school library for leisure reading, viewing, or listening		
8. Recognize the contribution of the school library program to the educational process		
9. Show enthusiasm about using the school library		
10. Have adequate access to the school library		
11. Learn to use a variety of school library technologies to access, use, and communicate information		
The School Librarian in Our School	**What Is**	**What Should Be**
1. Plays an active role in the teaching and learning process		
2. Collaborates with teachers to identify and teach information literacy skills and a research process		
3. Recognizes the leadership role of the building principal in developing an integrated school library and instructional program		
4. Recognizes his or her role as a leader for the school library program		
5. Has adequate knowledge of the curriculum being taught in classrooms		
6. Collaborates with teachers in the selection and/or development of resources to support instructional units		
7. Facilitates the use of school library resources and equipment to support classroom instruction		
8. Promotes the involvement of school library staff, materials, equipment, and facilities for teaching and learning		
9. Models and helps staff develop competencies in using school library resources and technologies		
10. Consults staff regarding areas of expertise (e.g., copyright, censorship, literature, reading, technology)		

Table 1.14 School Library Program Needs Assessment (*Continued*)

The School Librarian in Our School	What Is	What Should Be
11. Collaborates with teachers to teach students reference skills in a variety of formats (e.g., use of encyclopedias, magazine indexes, online resources, CD-ROM)		
12. Communicates with staff and students about new acquisitions available for their use		
13. Serves on district curriculum committees		
Classroom Teachers in Our School	**What Is**	**What Should Be**
1. Recognize the value of school library resources and technologies in relationship to teaching and learning		
2. Become familiar with available school library resources pertinent to subject area and/or grade level		
3. Give the school library staff information on topics to be covered in instructional units, as appropriate		
4. Participate in the selection of school library materials and equipment		
5. Collaborate with the school librarian in the development of instructional units that use school library resources and integrate information literacy skills, as appropriate		
6. Teach students reference skills (e.g., use of encyclopedias, magazine indexes)		
7. Instruct students through using a variety of school library resources, as appropriate		
8. Encourage students' independence in locating, using, and evaluating information from a variety of school library resources		
9. Provide time for students to gain access to school library resources		
10. Have adequate access to the school library		
Administrators in Our School	**What Is**	**What Should Be**
1. Recognize the contribution the school library program can make to the teaching/learning process		
2. Allocate sufficient building funds to school library resources and technologies that support the instructional program		
3. Encourage classroom teachers to become aware of available school library resources and technologies		
4. Encourage the school librarian to become aware of all curricular areas		

(Continued)

Table 1.14 School Library Program Needs Assessment (*Continued*)

Administrators in Our School	What Is	What Should Be
5. Involve the school librarian in curricular planning at the building, department, and/or team levels		
6. Encourage collaborative planning and teaching between teachers and school librarians that integrate information literacy skills and inquiry within the curriculum		
7. Provide time for collaborative instructional planning between teachers and school librarians		
8. Provide for building-level in-services related to school library resources and services		
9. Encourage integration of information literacy skills with classroom instruction		

Adapted from assessment tools developed by ESU #18 Evaluation Team for the Lincoln Public Schools Library Media Services Department.

PERSONAL AND PROFESSIONAL DEVELOPMENT

Personal professional development is the commitment of the school librarian to lifelong learning and is essential for maintaining and developing necessary leadership skills and staying abreast of current trends in education and the school library field. Many strategies may be used in pursuit of lifelong learning: professional learning networks, college and university courses, school district in-service programs, professional conferences, professional and other organizations, reading, viewing, listening, independent study, mentors, role models, membership webinars, commercially developed workshops, seminars, colloquia, and other continuing education activities.

This checklist (Table 1.15) is designed to assist the school librarian in identifying areas for personal professional development and formulating a plan for improving expertise. It is divided into five parts: (1) leader, (2) instructional partner, (3) information specialist, (4) teacher, and (5) program administrator. When pursuing professional development, school librarians should consider the attitudes and dispositions reflected in *Empowering Learners: Guidelines for School Librarians* (AASL 2009b) and *Standards for the 21st-Century Learner in Action* (AASL 2009a) and how they should also be incorporated into the roles of the school librarian.

Table 1.15 Professional Development for the School Librarian

Part 1. Leader

Rating Scale
- 0 Nonexistent
- 1 Poor
- 2 Fair
- 3 Good
- 4 Excellent

Identify areas for your personal and professional development using the rating scale above.

Leadership	0	1	2	3	4
Participation in school and district functions					
Participation in professional organizations					
Participation in community organizations					
Participation in political activities					
Participation on curriculum committees					
Participation on building committees					
Advocacy planning					
Communication					

Choose at least one item from those listed above and develop a plan for improving your expertise in that area.

My goal is to _____

_____

What strategies will you use to achieve your goal?

1. _____ 3. _____

2. _____ 4. _____

What human, financial, and material resources will you use?

1. _____ 3. _____

2. _____ 4. _____

When do you expect to complete your plan? _____

_____

How will you know when you have reached your goal? _____

_____

How will you reward yourself for completing your plan? _____

_____

Table 1.15 Professional Development for the School Librarian (*Continued*)

Part 2. Instructional Partner

Rating Scale
  0 **Nonexistent**
  1 **Poor**
  2 **Fair**
  3 **Good**
  4 **Excellent**

Identify areas for your personal and professional development using the rating scale above.

Collaborative Planning	0	1	2	3	4
Developing performance objectives					
Analyzing learner characteristics					
Developing assessment strategies for student learning					
Evaluating present learning activities					
Identifying information literacy skills					
Developing lesson strategy					
Selecting resources					
Scheduling classes or groups of students					
Establishing timelines					
Flexible use of school library					
Allocating space					
Identifying responsibilities					
Determining types of assessment: before, during, and after lesson					
Evaluating performance					
Revising lesson					
Curriculum Development	**0**	**1**	**2**	**3**	**4**
Selection of materials					
Acquisition of materials					
Utilization of materials					
Production of materials					
Evaluation of materials and services					
Curriculum Trends	**0**	**1**	**2**	**3**	**4**
Instruction for multiple literacies					
Instruction for research and inquiry					
Use of new technologies for instruction and learning					

Table 1.15 Professional Development for the School Librarian (*Continued*)

Choose at least one item from those listed above and develop a plan for improving your expertise in that area.

My goal is to _____

_____

What strategies will you use to achieve your goal?

1. _____ 3. _____

2. _____ 4. _____

What human, financial, and material resources will you use?

1. _____ 3. _____

2. _____ 4. _____

When do you expect to complete your plan? _____

_____

How will you know when you have reached your goal? _____

_____

How will you reward yourself for completing your plan? _____

_____

Part 3. Information Specialist

Rating Scale
- 0   Nonexistent
- 1   Poor
- 2   Fair
- 3   Good
- 4   Excellent

Identify areas for your personal and professional development using the rating scale above.

Collection Development	0	1	2	3	4
Children's materials					
Young adult materials					
Professional materials					
Equipment					
Online circulation, cataloging, acquisition					
Online databases/collections, reference resources					
Multiple Literacies (Information, Media, Visual, Technology)	**0**	**1**	**2**	**3**	**4**
Guidance in obtaining and using, evaluating, and communicating information					
Guidance in learning an inquiry research process					
Online catalog searching					
Internet searching					

Table 1.15 Professional Development for the School Librarian (*Continued*)

Multiple Literacies (Information, Media, Visual, Technology)	0	1	2	3	4
Guidance technology-assisted communication tools					
Database searching					
Copyright awareness					
Regard for privacy					
Regard for intellectual freedom					
Guidance in ethical use of information					
Resource evaluation					
Use of Web 2.0 tools					
Production	0	1	2	3	4
Audiovisual					
Television					
Computer-assisted instruction					
Desktop publishing					
Multimedia production					
Use of materials, equipment, and technologies					
Hardware and Software Management	0	1	2	3	4
Maintenance of materials and equipment					
Facilitating network resources					
Satellite and other technologies					
Troubleshooting hardware problems					
Troubleshooting software problems					
Installing software					
Facilitating online access					
Facilitating network access					

Choose at least one item from those listed above and develop a plan for improving your expertise in that area.

My goal is to _____

_____

What strategies will you use to achieve your goal?

1. _____ 3. _____

2. _____ 4. _____

What human, financial, and material resources will you use?

1. _____ 3. _____

2. _____ 4. _____

Table 1.15 Professional Development for the School Librarian (*Continued*)

When do you expect to complete your plan? _____
_____

How will you know when you have reached your goal? _____
_____

How will you reward yourself for completing your plan? _____
_____

Part 4. Teacher

Rating Scale
- 0   Nonexistent
- 1   Poor
- 2   Fair
- 3   Good
- 4   Excellent

Identify areas for your personal and professional development using the rating scale above.

Analyzing Learners	0	1	2	3	4
Developmental levels					
Learning styles: differentiated instruction					
Personal interests and needs					
Methods/Strategy	0	1	2	3	4
Collaborative Planning and Teaching					
Lecture					
Collaborative planning					
Discussion					
Demonstration					
Drill, practice, recitation					
Field trip					
Role-playing					
Games and simulations					
Reading/independent study					
Projects					
Programmed instruction					
Graphic organizers					
Rubrics					
Learning centers					
Expository					
Inquiry/discovery					

Table 1.15 Professional Development for the School Librarian (*Continued*)

Analyzing Learners	0	1	2	3	4
Problem solving					
Critical thinking					
Inquiry model approach					
Effective Lessons	0	1	2	3	4
Focusing attention					
Performance objectives					
Purpose					
Modeling					
Monitoring					
Adjusting					
Guided practice					
Independent practice					
Motivating Students	0	1	2	3	4
Integration with curriculum					
Interest					
Novelty/variety					
Involvement					
Level of concern					
Feeling tone					
Formative assessment					
Constructive criticism					
Difficulty level					
Prompts					
Behavioral Management/Discipline	0	1	2	3	4
Positive reinforcement of appropriate behavior					
Signaling progress					
Variety of positive reinforcement					
Appropriate schedules of reinforcement					
Negative consequences for inappropriate behavior					
Following negative reinforcement with positive reinforcement					
Specificity in reinforcement					
Learning climate					
Classroom management					

Table 1.15 Professional Development for the School Librarian (*Continued*)

Assessment	0	1	2	3	4
Aligned to standards: local, state, national					
Constructing test items					
Observation					
Rubrics					
Peer evaluation					
Summative assessment					
Self-assessment					
Strategies					

Choose at least one item from those listed above and develop a plan for improving your expertise in that area.

My goal is to _____

_____

What strategies will you use to achieve your goal?

1. _____ 3. _____

2. _____ 4. _____

What human, financial, and material resources will you use?

1. _____ 3. _____

2. _____ 4. _____

When do you expect to complete your plan? _____

_____

How will you know when you have reached your goal? _____

_____

How will you reward yourself for completing your plan? _____

_____

Part 5. Program Administrator

Rating Scale
   0   **Nonexistent**
   1   **Poor**
   2   **Fair**
   3   **Good**
   4   **Excellent**

Identify areas for your personal and professional development using the rating scale above.

Planning	0	1	2	3	4
Collaboration					
Needs assessment					
Forecasting/predicting					
Standards/guidelines					

Table 1.15 Professional Development for the School Librarian (*Continued*)

Planning	0	1	2	3	4
Mission, goals, and objectives					
Policy making					
Developing procedures					
Long range					
Setting priorities					
Decision making					
Action plans					
Organizing					
Staffing	0	1	2	3	4
Job description/analysis/evaluation					
Staff development/in-service education					
Performance appraisal					
Discipline/grievances					
Directing Motivation Theories/Leading	0	1	2	3	4
Developing and using power					
Consensus formulation					
Partnerships and coalitions					
Parliamentary procedures					
Persuading/influencing/advocacy					
Creative problem solving					
Risk taking					
Leadership theories					
Making connections, correlations					
Developing partnerships with stakeholders					
Communicating	0	1	2	3	4
Written					
Verbal					
Nonverbal					
Group dynamics					
Active listening					
Public relations					
Marketing					

Table 1.15 Professional Development for the School Librarian (*Continued*)

Communicating	0	1	2	3	4
Interpersonal relations					
Controlling/monitoring					
Standards/measurement/corrections					
Evaluations and assessment					
Cost benefit analysis					
Time and motion study					
Operations research					
Budgeting					
Facilities Planning and Use	0	1	2	3	4
Physical and virtual space (24-7 access)					
Ethics	0	1	2	3	4
Promotion of the right of intellectual freedom					
Copyright guidelines					
Equitable access					
Ethical use of information					

Choose at least one item from those listed above and develop a plan for improving your expertise in that area.

My goal is to _____

_____

What strategies will you use to achieve your goal?

1. _____ 3. _____

2. _____ 4. _____

What human, financial, and material resources will you use?

1. _____ 3. _____

2. _____ 4. _____

When do you expect to complete your plan? _____

_____

How will you know when you have reached your goal? _____

_____

How will you reward yourself for completing your plan? _____

_____

Adapted from *Information Power: Building Partnerships for Learning*, by the American Association of School Librarians, a division of the American Library Association, copyright © 1998, American Library Association. Used with permission.

REFERENCES

American Association of School Librarians. *AASL Standards for the 21st-Century Learner in Action*. Chicago: American Library Association, 2009a.

American Association of School Librarians. *Empowering Learners: Guidelines for School Library Media Programs*. Chicago: American Library Association, 2009b.

Zmuda, Allison. 2007. "Hitch Your Wagon to a Mission Statement." *School Library Media Activities Monthly* 24, No. 1 (September): 24–26.

ADDITIONAL READING

Adams, Helen R. *Ensuring Intellectual Freedom and Access to Information in the School Library Media Program*. Westport: Libraries Unlimited, 2008.

American Association of School Librarians. *AASL Standards for the 21st-Century Learner*. Chicago: American Library Association, 2007. http.//www.ala.org/aasl/standards/.

Anderson, Cyndee. *District Library Administration: A Big Picture Approach*. Worthington: Linworth, 2005.

Anderson, Cyndee, and Kathi Knop. *Write Grants Get Money*. 2nd ed. Worthington: Linworth, 2008.

Bennis, Warren. *On Becoming a Leader*. New York: Basic Books, 2009.

Bishop, Kay, and Sue Janczak. *A Staff Development Guide to Workshops for Technology and Information Literacy: Ready to Present!* Worthington: Linworth, 2005.

Bush, Gail. *The School Buddy System: The Practice of Collaboration*. Chicago: ALA Editions, 2003.

Bush, Gail. *School Library Media Programs in Action: Civic Engagement, Social Justice, and Equity*. Chicago: ALA Editions, 2009.

Bush, Gail, and Jami Biles Jones. *Tales Out of the School Library: Developing Professional Dispositions*. Santa Barbara: Libraries Unlimited, 2009.

Butler, Rebecca P. *Smart Copyright Compliance for Schools*. New York: Neal-Schuman, 2009.

Buzzeo, Toni. *The Collaborative Handbook*. Worthington: Linworth, 2008.

Carr, JoAnn. *Leadership for Excellence: Insights of National School Library Media Program of the Year Award Winners*. Chicago: American Library Association, 2008.

Coatney, Sharon, ed. *The Many Faces of School Library Leadership*. Santa Barbara: Libraries Unlimited, 2010.

Dickinson, Gail. *Empty Pockets and Full Plates: Effective Budget Administration for Library Media Specialists*. Worthington: Linworth, 2003.

Dickinson, Gail. *Portfolio Guide for School Library Media Specialists*. Chicago: ALA Editions, 2004.

Doll, Carol A., and Beth Doll. *The Resilient School Library Media Center*. Santa Barbara: Libraries Unlimited, 2010.

Downs, Elizabeth. *The School Library Media Specialist's Policy and Procedure Writer.* New York: Neal-Schuman, 2009.

Everhart, Nancy. *Controversial Issues in School Librarianship: Divergent Perspectives.* Worthington: Linworth, 2003.

Farmer, Leslie. *The Neal-Schuman Technology Management Handbook for School Library Media Centers.* New York: Neal-Schuman, 2010.

Fontichiaro, Kristina, ed. *21st-Century Learning in School Libraries.* Santa Barbara: Libraries Unlimited, 2009.

Foust, J'aimé L. *A Time Management and Organization Guide for School Librarians.* Worthington: Linworth, 2002.

Gilmore-See, Janice. *Simply Indispensable: An Action Guide for School Librarians.* Santa Barbara: Libraries Unlimited, 2010.

Gordon, Carol A. *Teaching and Learning in 21st Century School Libraries.* Santa Barbara: Libraries Unlimited, forthcoming.

Hall-Ellis, Sylvia D., and Ann Jarabek. *Grants for School Libraries.* Westport: Libraries Unlimited, 2004.

Hartsell, Gary. *Building Influence for the School Librarian.* 2nd ed. Worthington: Linworth, 2003.

Hauser, Judy. *The Web and Parents: Are You Tech Savvy?* Santa Barbara: Libraries Unlimited, 2009.

Heath, Marilyn S. *Electronic Portfolios: A Guide to Professional Development and Assessment.* Worthington: Linworth, 2004.

Hill, Ann, and Julieta Dias Fisher. *Tooting Your Own Horn: Web-Based Public Relations for the 21st Century Librarian.* Worthington: Linworth, 2002.

Howard, Jody K., and Su A. Eckhardt. *Action Research: A Guide for Library Media Specialists.* Worthington: Linworth, 2005.

Hughes-Hassell, Sandra, and Violet H. Harada. *School Reform and the School Library Media Specialist.* Westport: Libraries Unlimited, 2007.

Jones, Jami Biles, and Alana M. Zambone. *The Power of the Media Specialist to Improve Academic Achievement and Strengthen At-Risk Students.* Worthington: Linworth, 2008.

Junion-Metz, Gail, and Derrik Metz. *Instant Web Forms and Surveys for Children's/YA and School Libraries.* New York: Neal-Schuman, 2002.

Kuhlthau, Carol Collier, ed. *Assessment and the School Library Media Center.* Englewood: Libraries Unlimited, 1994.

Landau, Herbert B. *Winning the Library Grants: A Game Plan.* Chicago: ALA Editions, 2010.

Lankford, Mary. *Leadership and the School Librarian: Essays from Leaders in the Field.* Worthington: Linworth, 2006.

Lanning, Scott, and John Bryner. *Essential Reference Services for Today's School Media.* Santa Barbara: Libraries Unlimited, 2009.

LaPerriere, Jenny. *Merchandising Made Simple: Using Standards and Dynamite Displays to Boost Circulation.* Westport: Libraries Unlimited, 2008.

Lerman, James, et al. *Retool Your School.* Eugene: ISTE, 2010.

MacDonell, Colleen. *Essential Documents for School Libraries: "I've Got-It" Answers to "I-Need-It-Now" Questions.* Worthington: Linworth, 2005.

Markles, Sharon, ed. *The Innovative School Librarian.* New York: Neal-Schuman, 2009.

Martin, Ann M. *Seven Steps to an Award-Winning School Library Program.* Santa Barbara: Libraries Unlimited, 2010.

Martin, Barbara Stein, and Marco Zannier. *Fundamentals of School Library Media Management.* New York: Neal-Schuman, 2009.

Miller, Donna, and Karen Larsen. *Day-by-Day: Professional Journaling for Library Media Specialists.* Worthington: Linworth, 2003.

Morris, Betty J., et al. *Administering the School Library Media Center.* 5th ed. Santa Barbara: Libraries Unlimited, 2010.

Nichols, Beverly. *Improving Student Achievement: 50 More Research-Based Strategies for Educators.* Santa Barbara: Linworth, 2009.

Office of Intellectual Freedom. *Intellectual Freedom Manual.* 8th ed. Chicago: American Library Association, 2010.

Peters, Laurence. *Global Education.* Eugene: ISTE, 2009.

Reed, Sally Gardner. *Making the Case for Your School Library.* New York: Neal-Schuman, 2001.

Repman, Judi, and Gail Dickinson, eds. *School Library Management.* 6th ed. Worthington: Linworth, 2007. (7th ed., forthcoming)

Scales, Pat. *Protecting Intellectual Freedom in Your School Library.* Chicago: ALA Editions, 2009.

Scheeren, William O. *Technology for the School Librarian.* Santa Barbara: Libraries Unlimited, 2010.

Schuckett, Sandy. *Political Advocacy for School Librarians: You Have the Power!* Worthington: Linworth, 2004.

Schultz-Jones, Barbara. *An Automation Primer for School Library Media Centers.* Worthington: Linworth, 2006.

Small, Ruth. *Designing Digital Literacy Programs with IM-PACT.* New York: Neal-Schumann, 2005.

Stein, Barbara L., and Risa W. Brown. *Running a School Library Media Center: A How-to-Do-It Manual for Librarians.* New York: Neal-Schuman, 2002.

Stephens, Claire G., and Pat Franklin. *Library 101.* Westport: Libraries Unlimited, 2007.

Trilling, Bernie. *21st Century Skills: Learning for Life in Our Times.* San Francisco: Jossey-Bass, 2009.

Tuccillo, Diane P. *Teen-Centered Library Service: Putting Youth Participation into Practice.* Santa Barbara: Libraries Unlimited, 2009.

Valenza, Joyce Kasman. *Power Tools Recharged: 125+ Essential Forms and Presentations for Your School Library Information Program.* Chicago: ALA Editions, 2004.

Warlck, David F. *Redefining Literacy 2.0.* Worthington: Linworth, 2008.

Woolls, Blanche. *The School Library Media Manager.* Westport: Libraries Unlimited, 2008.

Zmuda, Allison, and Violet H. Harada. *Librarians as Learning Specialists Meeting the Learning Imperative for the 21st Century.* Westport: Libraries Unlimited, 2008.

Online Resources

American Association of School Librarians. "Issues and Advocacy." http://www.ala.org/ala/mgrps/divs/aasl/aaslissues/issuesadvocacy.cfm.

"Copyright for Teachers and School Librarians." http://users.mhc.edu/facultystaff/awalter/brim%20site/index.html.

2

Preparation of School Library Professionals

RATIONALE

Today's 21st-century schools need school library professionals who are certified, master teachers with an additional endorsement in school library that prepares them to direct school library programs that enable students to achieve the American Association of School Librarians (AASL; 2007) *AASL Standards for the 21st-Century Learner*. In *Empowering Learners*, AASL guidelines state that students should

1. inquire, think critically, and gain knowledge
2. draw conclusions, make informed decisions, apply knowledge to new situations, and create new knowledge
3. share knowledge and participate ethically and productively as members of our democratic society
4. pursue personal and aesthetic growth (AASL 2007, 14)

ACCREDITED, APPROVED, AND RECOGNIZED SCHOOL LIBRARY EDUCATION PROGRAMS

In most states, school librarians must have or acquire a current teaching certificate and an additional school library endorsement to direct a school library program. To ensure the school library is directed by qualified professionals, it is recommended that teaching credentials and endorsements be acquired from colleges and universities whose programs are accredited by the American Library Association (ALA)-AASL, the National Council for the Accreditation of Teacher Education, and/or their respective states' departments of education.

1. A complete list of programs that have been reviewed and approved by AASL's program reviewers using the ALA-AASL *Standards for Initial Programs for School Library Media Specialist Preparation* is available on the AASL Web site at http://www.ncate.org/documents/ProgramStandards/ala%202001.pdf.

2. A complete list of school library programs approved through state departments of education can be found by searching the list of state departments of education at http://wdcrobcolp01.ed.gov/Programs/EROD/org_list. cfm?category_ID=SEA/.

The following are the endorsement requirements established for Nebraska. Requirements vary from state to state and can be found at http://www.schoollibrarymonthly. com/cert/index.html.

NEBRASKA SCHOOL LIBRARY ENDORSEMENT REQUIREMENTS (RULE 24)

006.37A Library Media Specialist

006.37B Endorsement Type: Field

006.37C Persons with this endorsement may supervise the development and the organization of a library media program and teach or direct the use of the library media resources and services in kindergarten through grade 12.

00637D Certificate Endorsement Requirements: This endorsement shall require the applicant to hold a teaching certificate or concurrently earn a subject or field endorsement, and acquire a minimum of 30 semester hours in library media courses, including administration, technology, organization of resources, information access, children and young adult literature, selection and curriculum and instruction.

006.37E Endorsement Program Requirements: Nebraska teacher education institutions offering this endorsement program must have on file, within the institution, a plan which identifies the courses and the course completion requirements which the institution utilizes to grant credit toward completion of this endorsement.

Candidates in Nebraska school library media program will develop the skills and dispositions that enhance their ability to:

a. Demonstrate a commitment to personal professional growth, including being able to:

 1. Exhibit comprehension of the role of libraries in a democratic society and the interrelationships of all types of libraries and information agencies;
 2. Exhibit an understanding of the role of the school library media program as a central element in the intellectual life of the school;
 3. Advocate and promote opportunities to improve the profession both independently and collectively;
 4. Engage in continuous self-evaluation and self-directed learning for personal professional growth;
 5. Demonstrate a knowledge of appropriate local, state, regional, and national professional associations, guidelines, and publications;
 6. Demonstrate a knowledge of legal regulations regarding intellectual property rights and educational fair use guidelines of the copyright law;
 7. Demonstrate a knowledge of means for promoting intellectual freedom;

8. Demonstrate a knowledge of professional ethics;
9. Exhibit comprehension of the importance of cooperation and networking among libraries and other information agencies;
10. Identify legislation and policy at the local, state, and national levels that affect the development of the school library media programs and take appropriate action; and,
11. Use systematic practices for researching existing and emerging applications of technology as they impact the library media program.

b. Demonstrate the ability to communicate effectively with elementary, middle level, and secondary students, faculty, staff, administrators, school boards, parents, and other members of the community, including being able to:

1. Create a positive teaching and learning climate in the school library media center;
2. Listen and respond to information requests in a manner that encourages further patron inquiry;
3. Practice effective interpersonal relationships within as well as outside the school community and communicate regularly to further school goals and relate library media program needs and accomplishments;
4. Exhibit communication skills necessary for collaborative planning of curriculum and lessons with teachers, i.e., the ability to demonstrate an understanding of curriculum objectives, to listen effectively, to use probing and clarifying questions, and to negotiate responsibility for activities;
5. Develop and implement an effective public relations program that communicates the vital contribution of the school library media program to learning; and,
6. Use technology to communicate information and ideas.

c. Apply basic principles of evaluating and selecting resources to build and maintain a collection that includes access to internal and external resources to support the educational mission of the district, including being able to:

1. Create and implement selection and collection development policies and procedures that reflect the district's mission;
2. Develop criteria for evaluating resources at all grade levels;
3. Use collection management principles and procedures for needs assessment, evaluating, selecting, and discarding resources;
4. Evaluate internal and external resources; and,
5. Apply systematic techniques in maintaining resources to support personal development, curriculum, multi-cultural, and life-long learning needs of students, faculty, staff, and administration.

d. Develop a library media program that provides access to information and ideas, including being able to:

1. Develop and monitor services and policies that ensure equitable and unrestricted access to information and ideas in all formats and for all ability levels;

2. Develop and monitor a formal process for addressing expressed concerns about library media resources;

3. Communicate concepts pertinent to information access; and,

4. Develop and monitor policies and procedures to protect confidentiality and privacy of library media center users.

e. Use resources to support the information needs of elementary, middle level, and secondary students, and the instructional development needs of faculty, including being able to:

1. Develop a partnership with faculty to ensure that the evaluation and selection process provides curriculum-related resources appropriate to learner characteristics such as abilities, interests, needs, and learning styles;

2. Ensure that the evaluation and selection process provides curriculum-related resources that reflect instructional strategies, and learning and teaching styles; and,

3. Recognize the characteristics unique to each information format and select items according to their specific contribution to learning objectives or personal, developmental needs.

f. Assist elementary, middle level, and secondary students and faculty to design and produce resources using current technology, including being able to:

1. Analyze criteria to determine the appropriateness of producing local resources as opposed to selecting commercially produced resources;

2. Apply basic principles of instructional design in developing, producing, and implementing technological resources for a specified learning objective; and,

3. Apply evaluative criteria for locally produced media for inclusion in the collection.

g. Implement policies and procedures for the acquisition, cataloging, processing, circulating, and maintaining resources to ensure access, including being able to:

1. Coordinate the acquisition process for resources, technology, equipment, and supplies;

2. Implement standard recognized procedures for classifying, cataloging, and processing resources that will facilitate computerization and resource sharing;

3. Organize and maintain current bibliographic records;

4. Select appropriate systems for circulation and access;

5. Implement and evaluate circulation policies and procedures based on needs of users; and,

6. Implement procedures for ongoing inventory and maintenance of resources.

h. Work with elementary, middle level, and secondary students, faculty, staff, administrators, and members of the community to develop, implement, and evaluate library media programs to meet educational goals, including the management of personnel, resources, services, and facilities, including being able to:

1. Demonstrate an understanding of how to establish library media program goals within district policies;
2. Develop annual and long-range plans to meet the goals of a library media program and disseminate those plans to individuals and groups;
3. Interpret and support school and district policies and regulations;
4. Apply effective management principles to the administration of the school library media program;
5. Design, establish and communicate policies and procedures for the implementation of an effective library media program;
6. Prepare, justify and administer the library media program budget based on instructional program needs;
7. Participate in planning, scheduling (including flexible scheduling), and using library media facilities to support the instructional program;
8. Supervise, assign, instruct, and assist in the evaluation of support staff, volunteers, and student assistants;
9. Collaborate with others to provide increased access to information through resource sharing;
10. Evaluate the instructional effects of the library media program;
11. Apply appropriate research findings to improve teaching and learning through the library media program;
12. Conduct action research to assist in the development and implementation of an effective library media program;
13. Monitor, assess, and employ existing and emerging technologies for management and instructional applications;
14. Demonstrate a knowledge of how technology is used to connect information sources among users both locally and globally;
15. Utilize and facilitate the efforts of a library media advisory committee; and,
16. Participate in school-wide instruction leadership efforts, including being able to train library media staff and faculty in library media programs, processes and procedures, including technology, resources, equipment, and services.

i. Serve as a learning facilitator within schools and as a leader of faculty, administration, and elementary, middle level, and secondary students in the development of effective strategies for teaching and learning, including being able to:

1. Cooperatively plan with other faculty to ensure that information literacy skills are taught and practiced as curriculum integrated learning experiences, including retrieving, analyzing, interpreting, organizing, evaluating, synthesizing, and communicating information and ideas;
2. Demonstrate an understanding of how to participate, as an educational leader, an equal partner, and a change agent in the curriculum development process at both the building and district levels;

3. Work with other faculty to identify appropriate instructional strategies and creative uses of resources;

4. Collaboratively plan with other faculty to provide activities and opportunities for students to assume responsibilities for planning, undertaking, and assuming independent learning;

5. Anticipate the need for specific information and resources in response to information needs identified in the curriculum development process;

6. Share with other faculty the role of teacher, motivator, coach, and guide for students in the development of reading, listening, and viewing competencies, including critical thinking skills, for lifelong learning;

7. Motivate and guide students in appreciating literature;

8. Collaboratively plan with other faculty in designing, evaluating, and modifying teaching and learning activities, and in evaluating student mastery of these activities;

9. Assist students and faculty in developing independence in retrieving, analyzing, interpreting, organizing, evaluating, synthesizing, and communicating information and ideas;

10. Design production activities, including adapting resources for new purposes, to assist in the development of skills for analyzing, evaluating, synthesizing, and communicating information; and,

11. Plan and implement staff development activities to increase competence in locating, using, and producing resources for teaching and professional growth (Nebraska State Board of Education 2008, 155–160)

NATIONAL BOARD PROFESSIONAL TEACHING STANDARDS

The National Board for Professional Teaching Standards (NBPTS) represent a "professional consensus on the critical aspects of practice that distinguish accomplished library media specialists" (NBPTS 2001). The 10 NBPTS standards for library media specialists identify "the essential knowledge, skills, dispositions, and commitments that allow library media specialists to practice at a high level" (NBPTS 2001). The standards are as follows.

What Library Media Specialists Know

   I. Knowledge of Learners
  II. Knowledge of Teaching and Learning
 III. Knowledge of Library and Information: What Library Media Specialists Do
  IV. Integrating Instruction
   V. Leading Innovation through the Library Media Program
  VI. Administering the Library Media Program: How Library Media Specialists Grow as Professionals
 VII. Reflective Practice
VIII. Professional Growth
  IX. Ethics, Equity, and Diversity
   X. Leadership, Advocacy, and Community Partnerships (NBPTS 2001)

School library media professionals who wish to pursue an NBPTS certificate should

1. review procedures and portfolio guidelines available on the NBPTS Web site at http://www.nbpts.org/for_candidates/certificate_areas1?ID=19&x= 28&y=11/
2. contact their school administrators and respective state departments of education to find information and financial resources for their NBPTS portfolio process as well as incentives for NBPTS certificate completion

Each of the documents cited in this chapter guides the education and professional performance of school librarians as well as the endorsement standards. These resources can inform school librarians, administrators, professors, and students interested in becoming school librarians about performance standards for quality school librarians and the school libraries they direct.

REFERENCES

American Association of School Librarians. 2007. *AASL Standards for the 21st-Century Learner.* http.//www.ala.org/aasl/standards.

National Board for Professional Teaching Standards. 2001. "Library Media/Early Childhood through Young Adulthood." http://www.nbpts.org/for_candidates/certificate_areas1?ID=19&x=28&y=11/.

Nebraska State Board of Education. 2008. "Rule 24: Library Media Specialist Endorsement Guidelines." http://www.nde.state.ne.us/LEGAL/COVER24.html.

ADDITIONAL READING

American Association of School Librarians. "Learning about the Job: What Does a School Library Media Specialist Do?" http://www.ala.org/ala/mgrps/divs/aasl/aasleducation/recruitmentlib/learningabout/learningabout.cfm.

American Association of School Librarians. "Nationally Recognized NCATE/AASL Reviewed and Approved School Library Media Education Programs." http://www.ala.org/ala/mgrps/divs/aasl/aasleducation/schoollibrarymed/ncateaaslreviewed.cfm.

American Library Association. "ALA and AASL: Assuring Quality in School Library Media Education Programs." http://www.ala.org/ala/mgrps/divs/aasl/aasleducation/school library/ncateaaslreviewed.cfm.

Institute for Library and Information Literacy Education. "Do Schools Need a Certified Library Media Specialist (LMS)?" http://www.ilile.org/initiatives/principal_project/Admin/3need.html.

U.S. Department of Education. "State Education Agency (State Department of Education)." http://wdcrobcolp01.ed.gov/Programs/EROD/org_list.cfm?category_ID=SEA/.

3

Preparation and Training of School Library Paraprofessionals

RATIONALE

A credentialed school library professional directs a strong 21st-century school library program with assistance of school library paraprofessionals who provide assistance in the management of the daily operations of a school library. While school library paraprofessionals often provide valuable support for and/or are directly involved in student instruction, a paraprofessional's position is a nonteaching position with a focus on clerical and technical activities key to the maintenance of a high-quality school library program. In *Empowering Learners*, AASL guidelines state that "the school library media program has a minimum of one full-time certificated/licensed library media specialist support by qualified staff sufficient for the school's instructional programs, services, facilities, size, and number of teachers and students" (AASL 2009, 32).

Titles of school library paraprofessionals may vary, for example, library assistant, library technician, library associate, library clerk, and library aide, but regardless of title, school library paraprofessionals are involved in a diverse array of activities that may include the following:

1. maintenance of print and digital information resources, that is, processing, mending, and shelving according to established standards
2. management/clerical activities involving records, forms, and other communication with teachers, administrators, parents, and community stakeholders
3. maintenance of an organized and inviting school library facility
4. technical support for audiovisual and other instructional formats
5. supervision of student assistants and parent/community volunteers
6. access to support in cooperation with the school librarian to assist students, teachers, administrators, parents, and community stakeholders in locating and using information resources for academic and personal pursuits

TRAINING AND EDUCATION FOR SCHOOL LIBRARY PARAPROFESSIONALS

States may require education and training for paraprofessionals who work in schools. For example, Nebraska has two education/training venues for professional development for public librarians. But the knowledge, skills, and dispositions emphasized in the course work are relevant to the work of paraprofessionals in all genres of libraries. For school library paraprofessionals who wish to acquire or enhance skills related to services, resources, and programming in school libraries, these options provide an affordable and accessible educational venue.

Nebraska Library Commission Basic Skills

The Nebraska Library Commission basic skills program is composed of four courses, offered in a two-year rotation. The courses are held on-site in all six Nebraska Regional Library Systems in Nebraska and are also offered online. The basic skills training courses are as follows.

Library Administration

- Library Bill of Rights
- Intellectual Freedom Handbook
- Planning, Marketing, Advocacy
- Policies and Procedures
- Trustee Handbook
- Library Law
- Library Friends Groups and Foundations
- Management and Personnel
- Policies and Procedures
- Budgeting

Public Services

- Customer Service
- Dealing with Difficult Patrons
- Customers with Special Needs
- Reference
- Readers' Advisory
- Programming
- Outreach
- The Library Environment

Collection Development

- Collection Development Policies
- Community Needs Assessment
- Selection of Library Materials
- Acquisitions
- Weeding
- Intellectual Freedom
- Collection Assessment
- Preservation

Organization of Library Materials

- The Cataloging Process
- Classification Using the Dewey Decimal System
- Finding Catalogs and Catalog Records Online
- Evaluating Catalog Records

Nebraska Community College Library and Information Services Program

Central Community College, in cooperation with the Nebraska Library Commission and the University of Nebraska at Omaha, offers two options for library and information services students: (1) a certificate program in library and information services and (2) an associate of arts degree with an emphasis in library science.

Students who complete the 18 hours of library and information services courses will enhance their ability to do the following:

1. develop library programming
2. purchase and process all types of materials
3. plan and compile budgets
4. develop collection development and management plans
5. supervise library staff

Credits earned during the acquisition of the associate of arts degree may be considered as viable transfer courses in undergraduate degree programs in library science.

The resources listed in this chapter will help inform school librarians, school library nonprofessionals, and administrators about expectations and training options for school library–related responsibilities.

REFERENCES

American Association of School Librarians. 2009. "Position Statement on Appropriate Staffing for School Library Media Centers." http://www.ala.org/ala/mgrps/divs/aasl/aaslissues/positionstatements/appropriatestaffing.cfm.

ADDITIONAL READING

Central Community College. 2010. "Library and Information Services." http://www.cccneb. edu/igsbase/igstemplate.cfm?SRC=SP&SRCN=programchart2&GnavID=20&SnavID=& TnavID=&cccProgramID=176&LS=&PS=&KS=.

Nebraska Library Commission. 2009. "Basic Skills Training Courses." http://www.nlc.state. ne.us/libdev/basic.html.

4

School Library Personnel and Evaluation

RATIONALE

The 21st-century school library program is an integral part of the total educational program and serves students and faculty in meeting curricular goals. A staff of professional and support personnel are required to develop and maintain a high-quality program. "Staffing is structured to support teaching and learning throughout the school community. The numbers and skill sets of support staff and volunteers [depend] on the school's instructional programs, services, facilities, size and number of students and teachers [and the] . . . [school library media program] SMLP includes at least one full-time certificated or licensed school library media specialist [SLMS] to help integrate the program's missions and goals into all aspects of the school curricula" (American Association of School Librarians [AASL] 2009, 32). It is important to evaluate personnel to provide accountability, evidence of success, and direction for improvement.

GENERAL INFORMATION

A successful school library program depends on adequate professional and support staffing. Recommendations and requirements for preparation and certification of school library personnel can be found in chapters 2 and 3. In this chapter, a school library program duty profile is provided to indicate the involvement of the school library personnel in various assigned duties. Duties listed enable the user of this section to determine whether those assigned to staffing levels are performing appropriate duties. The suggested list of duties for school library staff is intended to be used as the basis of job descriptions. Examples of staff evaluation forms are included.

LEVELS AND PATTERNS OF STAFFING

Levels and patterns of staffing are dependent on a number of variables; these include the school's mission; size of the school; expectations of the faculty, administrators, and students; the integration of the school library program into the curriculum; and the relationship of student learning to school library services and resources. The curriculum, school organization, physical plant, special student populations, general staffing of the school, and services provided by the building, district, or regional school library programs are also critical elements in determining levels and patterns of staffing.

Although staffing patterns are developed to meet local needs, certain basic staffing requirements can be identified. They must reflect the following principles:

1. All students, teachers, and administrators in each school building at all grade levels must have access to a school library provided by at least one certificated school librarian working full time in the school library.
2. Both professional personnel and support staff are necessary for the school library program at all grade levels.
3. More than one school library professional is required in many schools. The number of additional professional staff is determined by the school's size, number of students and teachers, facilities, specific school library program components, and unique features of the school's instructional program.

Every state requires certain levels of staffing for the school library. For example, the current requirements for a school librarian in the state of Nebraska, according to Rule 10, are as follows:

007.04 Media/Technology Staff. Quality Indicator: The library/media/technology programs and services are an integral part of the instructional program. Library/media staff provide leadership and assistance in selection, provision, and use of library/media resources. Technology staff and services are available locally or in collaboration with other agencies to provide support, maintenance, consultation, and training for meaningful use of technology resources.

007.04A Each K–12 school system and each secondary school system has a person holding a Nebraska Teaching Certificate with an endorsement appropriate for library science or educational media specialist, or meeting Section 007.04B, assigned on at least a one-half time basis to provide library media services to the school system.

007.04A1 Each school building having an enrollment of from 70 to 249 students has a person holding a valid Nebraska Teaching Certificate with an appropriate endorsement for library science or educational media specialist assigned on at least a one-fifth time basis or has a library media paraprofessional assigned on at least a one-half time basis under the supervision of a certificated staff member.

007.04A2 Each school building having an enrollment of at least 250 students has a person holding a Nebraska Teaching Certificate with a specialist assigned on at least a one-half time basis, or has such person assigned on a one-fourth time basis and a full-time library media paraprofessional also assigned. Buildings with 500 or more students have at least a full-time educational media specialist or a one-half time educational media specialist and a full-time library media paraprofessional. Buildings with 750 or more students have a full-time educational media specialist.

007.04B Until September 1, 2010, a school system may assign a person holding a Nebraska Teaching Certificate with no endorsement appropriate for library science or educational media specialist to fulfill the requirements for Sections 007.04A, 007.04A1, and 007.04A2 if such person acquires at least six credit hours each year toward an appropriate endorsement pursuant to 92 NAC 24. Persons employed by a Nebraska school prior to July 1, 1989, to provide library media services and who hold a Nebraska Special Services Certificate with an endorsement appropriate for library media services may fulfill the requirements of these regulations. (Nebraska State Board of Education 2009, 21–22)

CERTIFICATED STAFF

The roles of the school librarian have been identified as leader, instructional partner, information specialist, teacher, and program administrator (AASL 2009, 16–18). These roles are defined in chapter 5 and addressed in chapter 1. Now and in the future, the school librarian must be a creative risk taker, with vision to transform a student-centered learning environment in a way that meets the needs of 21st-century learning and teaching. This type of program development requires a certificated school librarian who is continually learning and adapting to new resources and technologies.

Certificated School Librarian

Qualified and certificated school librarians always staff professional positions in the school library program. The school librarian must be prepared to act as the program administrator, responsible for the planning, development, implementation, and overall evaluation of the entire program. This responsibility includes supervision of other professionals, clerical, and support staff. The school librarian must meet state certification requirements as both a school librarian and a professional educator. The school librarian serves on curriculum and school improvement committees, is part of a management team, and coordinates the school library program.

The school librarian must have a broad undergraduate education with a liberal arts background and hold a master's degree or equivalent from a program that combines academic and professional preparation in library and information science, education, management, media, communications theory, and technology. Licensing by the appropriate state agency is also essential.

Other Professional Staff Involved in School Library Programs

Some school districts employ other educational professionals as technical staff. These professionals have additional experience in areas such as instructional technology or information technology. In addition to degrees in their specific disciplines, they have academic preparation in educational theory and methodology. It is important for the school librarian to work closely with technical staff in conjunction with the school library program.

NONCERTIFICATED STAFF

The school library program, regardless of size, needs an adequate level of support staff. The support staff works under the guidance and supervision of the professional school librarian and provides services that free the school librarian to work directly and closely with students and faculty in the school. Support staff also may interact directly with the school community, but their primary responsibilities are routine clerical and technical duties. Individual districts assign a variety of job titles to these staff members. A few common examples are school library paraprofessional, school library aide, school library clerk, school library associate, and school library technical assistant.

Student Assistants and Adult Volunteers

Additional assistance in the school library is often provided by volunteers and student's aides, although volunteers should not be considered as substitutes for trained, paid, noncertificated clerical and technical staff. Volunteers—parents, retired persons, or other community members—are available in some schools to assist in specific areas of the school library. Because they often possess unique talents, skills, and experiences, they are capable of providing services to supplement the work of the school librarian and the school library paraprofessional staff.

LIBRARY MEDIA DUTY PROFILE

This profile was developed to help the school librarian and school administrators define the roles and duties of certificated and noncertificated school library staff.

Table 4.1 Library Media Duty Profile

Building _____ Level _____ Enrollment _____ Staff _____

To plot the School Library Profile on the chart that follows, the user should indicate who performs the function listed on the left and the frequency with which it is performed.

Rating Scale
  1   **Frequently Performed**
  2   **Occasionally Performed**
  3   **Seldom Performed**
  4   **Not Performed**

CERTIFICATED SCHOOL LIBRARIAN DUTIES	Performed by Certificated School Librarian	Performed by Noncertificated Support Staff
Confers with administrators and/or school board concerning school library program operations, programs, and budgets		
Assists curriculum committees in selecting appropriate materials and school library program activities		
Cooperates in the development and implementation of proposals for federal projects, programs, and service units		

Table 4.1 Library Media Duty Profile (*Continued*)

CERTIFICATED SCHOOL LIBRARIAN DUTIES	Performed by Certificated School Librarian	Performed by Noncertificated Support Staff
Organizes the school library collection		
Reads and uses professional reviews of learning materials		
Develops short-term and long-term goals for the school library program		
Provides training, supervision, and performance evaluations of school library support staff		
Collaborates with teachers to coordinate school library program activities and resources with classroom units and instruction		
Acts as an instructional partner for students and teachers		
Provides and supports literature enrichment activities		
Keeps an up-to-date inventory of learning materials and equipment		
Maintains collection of learning materials and online services		
Helps students to develop good listening, viewing, reading, and technology habits		
Attends and participates in meetings of professional organizations		
Supplies bibliographical information		
Develops and supervises a distribution of materials system		
Weeds the collection		
Maintains the catalog		
Coordinates activities related to educational video transmission and recording (cable, satellite, downloading)		
Teaches students *Standards for the 21st-Century Learner* in collaboration with classroom teachers in the context of content-based lessons		
Instructs students in the selection and use of print resources and also in the use and evaluation of online and other digital resources		
Cooperates with other school librarians and librarians within the community and educational service units		
Participates in the planning and implementation of school staff development programs		
Coordinates public relations, marketing, and advocacy activities		

Table 4.1 Library Media Duty Profile (*Continued*)

CERTIFICATED SCHOOL LIBRARIAN DUTIES	Performed by Certificated School Librarian	Performed by Noncertificated Support Staff
Supervises the volunteer program		
Participates in the development of school and district policies, including materials selection policies, and online acceptable use policies		
Develops and maintains a procedures manual		
Promotes digital citizenship and responsible use of information and technology		
Oversees collection development, including selection of resources for the school library in collaboration with teachers and students		
Follows copyright policy and assists staff and students in understanding copyright laws, plagiarism, educational fair use, and intellectual freedom		
NONCERTIFICATED SCHOOL LIBRARY STAFF DUTIES		
Places orders for resources and checks them in		
Processes resources		
Shelves resources		
Orders and maintains an inventory of supplies		
Enters data for electronic catalogs		
Maintains the electronic or card catalog for inventory records of the collection		
Assists students and staff in finding resources		
Schedules and distributes equipment and learning materials		
Maintains and repairs equipment and learning materials		
Operates equipment such as computers and other digital tools		
Manages the circulation desk		
Prepares displays		
Assists with development of bibliographies		

METHODS OF EVALUATION: CERTIFICATED STAFF

Evaluation of the certificated school librarian is an important aspect of role clarification. Many of the responsibilities are unique to the position; therefore the methods used to evaluate the school librarian should be designed to reflect the job description. A variety of methods may be used to evaluate performance:

- goals
- dialogue/conference
- reports
- observation
- portfolios
- self-evaluation
- patrons
- survey instruments

The following is an example of a job description that could be used for the school librarian.

SAMPLE: SCHOOL LIBRARIAN JOB DESCRIPTION
Position Title:

School Librarian

Requirements:

Current Teaching Certificate with School Library Endorsement

Reports To:

Building Principal

Job Goals:

To promote the educational development of each student by organizing and maintaining a school library program that integrates information literacy, literature, and information technologies into the curriculum. The school librarian is a teacher, information specialist, instructional partner, program administrator, and leader (AASL 2009).

Duties and Responsibilities:

Manage and administer the school library program, including budget, collection development and maintenance, circulation system, and school library policies and procedures, within district guidelines.

Provide training, supervision, and input to performance evaluation of the noncertificated, clerical, and technical personnel in the school library program.

Serve as an information specialist on district curriculum committees and communicate and work cooperatively with other school librarians, both within the district and with other schools and agencies.

Keep current in areas of curriculum development, teaching methodology, program organization, and information as it relates to the school library media program.

Teach students 21st-century skills and promote reading as an essential skill.

Provide guidance to school personnel regarding copyright, principles of intellectual freedom, and ethical behavior as well as other laws and guidelines pertaining to the ownership, distribution, and use of resources.

Promote the use of technology to expand curriculum goals and support students in developing critical thinking and evaluation skills.

Maintain a current and varied collection of diverse resources, both digital and textual, that offer multiple perspectives and are aligned with the school's curriculum.

Collaborate with teachers and students to provide instruction, learning strategies, and practice in using the essential 21st-century learner skills.

Portfolio Evaluation

Although portfolios can be used for job interviews and for evaluating performance, the focus here is on using portfolios as an evaluation instrument. Portfolios must reflect a specific purpose, namely, to show evidence of growth and improvement, to reflect the purpose of evaluation, or to show the work of the school librarian. The following is a list of items that might be included in a portfolio; it is a sample of items that might be included rather than a comprehensive list:

- evidence of good teaching
- lesson plans
- student projects
- examples of student assessments
- forms used in collaborative planning
- video of lessons taught
- job description
- mission of the school library program
- goals of the school library program
- documentation of what has been done to achieve the goals
- photographs and visual documentation of activities
- photos of special displays and exhibits
- reports to administrators
- newsletters to teachers, administrators, or parents
- media coverage of events
- involvement in professional organizations
- awards or grants received
- flyers for special activities
- copies of policies developed
- work on curriculum committees
- publications
- professional involvement

SCHOOL LIBRARIAN PERFORMANCE: EXAMPLES OF SUMMATIVE EVALUATIONS

Following are samples of school librarian summative evaluations.

Table 4.2 School Librarian Summative Evaluation Sample Form

Name _____

School _____

Date _____

Evaluation Ratings:
- 3   **Exceeds Expectation**
- 2   **Meets Expectation**
- 1   **Needs Improvement**
- NA   **Not Applicable**

Performance Area	Rating	Comments
School Library Management and Administration		
Organizes and administers school library and program to promote and ensure efficient use by students and staff		
Trains and supervises school library personnel to perform duties efficiently		
Administers goals, objectives, policies, and procedures related to the school library		
Develops plans to meet information literacy and information technology needs of the school		
Instructional Process		
Promotes student achievement by working collaboratively with teachers to integrate information literacy and information technology skills into the curriculum		
Manages student behavior and promotes a positive environment		
Is knowledgeable in area of curriculum content and instructional methods		
Interpersonal Relationships		
Communicates and interacts in a professional manner with the school community		
Develops and maintains a working relationship with local, regional, and state library systems and promotes awareness and utilization of the systems with students and staff		
Professional Responsibilities		
Participates in professional growth activities		

Table 4.2 School Librarian Summative Evaluation Sample Form (*Continued*)

Performance Area	Rating	Comments
Follows district and building policies and procedures		
School Librarian Signature _____ Evaluator Signature _____ Date of Conference _____ The signature of the school librarian indicates that the evaluation conference has been held and that the school librarian has seen but does not necessarily concur with this report.		

Indicators of Effective School Librarians

(Adapted from Millard Public Schools, Omaha, Nebraska)

Table 4.3 Indicators of Effective School Librarians

Adapted from Millard Public Schools, Omaha, Nebraska

School Librarian _____   Date_____

Notes:

Indicators	Indicators/Description of Effective School Librarian	Satisfactory	Needs Improvement	Not Applicable
Planning	1.1 Works with classroom teacher and administrators to plan integrated information literacy and inquiry instruction			
	1.2 Seeks input from students and staff when planning collection purchases			
	1.3 Follows building and district guidelines for purchasing			
	1.4 Assists teachers in the preview and selection of information materials and tools for classroom activities			
Management	2.1 Trains and supervises paraprofessionals assigned to the school library			
	2.2 Maintains a balanced collection of print and electronic resources			
	2.3 Provides timely and accurate inventories, reports, and information			

Table 4.3 Indicators of Effective School Librarians (*Continued*)

Indicators	Indicators/Description of Effective School Librarian	Satisfactory	Needs Improvement	Not Applicable
	2.4 Supervises care of equipment and repair procedures			
	2.5 Manages time efficiently and maintains a flexible schedule in a business-like manner			
	2.6 Uses effective skills of communication in relating to parents, volunteers, and staff			
	2.7 Provides leadership in technology integration			
	2.8 Follows district selection policy which includes procedures for reconsideration of materials			
	2.9 Exhibits a pleasant, friendly, and cooperative attitude toward staff and students			
	2.10 Develops and maintains effective working relationships among school staff			
Instruction	3.1 Provides systematic instruction in information literacy skills			
	3.2 Communicates instructional objectives to students			
	3.3 Shows how present topic is related to topics that have been taught or will be taught			
	3.4 Relates subject topics to existing student experiences			
	3.5 Uses signaled responses, questioning techniques, and/or guided practices to involve all students			
	3.6 Teaches the objectives through a variety of methods			
	3.7 Gives directions that are clearly stated and related to the objectives			
	3.8 Demonstrates the desired skill or process			

Table 4.3 Indicators of Effective School Librarians (*Continued*)

Indicators	Description	Satisfactory	Needs Improvement	Not Applicable
	3.9 Checks to determine if students are progressing toward stated objectives			
	3.10 Uses principles of differentiation in instruction			
	3.11 Summarizes or fits into context what has been taught			
	3.12 Clearly defines expected student behavior			
	3.13 Treats students with respect and dignity			
Environment	4.1 Establishes and maintains a pleasant, safe, and orderly climate conducive to learning			
	4.2 Encourages students to develop lifelong reading, listening, and thinking skills			
	4.3 Publicizes programs, services, and materials through newsletters, announcements, and/or Web pages			
Assessment	5.1 Works with classroom teacher to assign grades and evaluate student work			
Professional Responsi- bility	6.1 Supports professional organiza- tions			
	6.2 Provides staff development in the area of technology/information integration			
	6.3 Serves on building and district committees for curriculum development and implementation			
	6.4 Adheres to district, department, and building policies			
Technology Support	7.1 Provides input to and assists in the implementation of technology at the building and district levels			

Table 4.3 Indicators of Effective School Librarians (*Continued*)

Indicators	Description	Satisfactory	Needs Improvement	Not Applicable
	7.2 Assists in the selection of appropriate materials, media, and supplies that support student learning and district curriculum			
	7.3 Assists in the planning, implementation, and evaluation of staff development for technology at the building level			
	7.4 Serves as a liaison between the building, staff, community and technology division			
	7.5 Knowledgeable about copyright, software licensing, and Internet filtering			
	7.6 Assists with technology setups, inventories, and troubleshoots technical problems			
	7.7 Knowledgeable in the use and backup of the building file server			
	7.8 Knowledgeable in the use of the district's WAN and the Internet			
	7.9 Assists in problem solving appropriate uses of technology in an educational setting			
	7.10 Collaborates with staff in the appropriate integration of technology into curriculum, instruction, and assessment to improve teaching and student learning			
	7.11 Works with site and district planning/advisory teams, as requested			
	7.12 Attends monthly meetings and training sessions, as requested			

JOB DESCRIPTIONS AND SAMPLE EVALUATIONS FOR NONCERTIFICATED STAFF

School Library Paraprofessional

Job Description
Suggested Duties and Responsibilities
Duties

a. supports the school librarian in providing quality services to students, teachers, and administrators
b. assists with the acquisition of new materials, for example, checks to see if requested titles are already in the collection, identifies vendors and prices, processes purchase orders, and transmits orders electronically
c. processes new materials and equipment, for example, ownership and condition, and inputs information into the school library electronic catalog
d. manages the distribution of resources and equipment, for example, circulation, overdues, and return of materials to their proper location
e. locates and retrieves materials and equipment as requested
f. assists students and teachers in using resources and equipment
g. supervises school library student assistants
h. prepares bibliographies and reports
i. assists with various record-keeping activities, for example, circulation and usage statistics
j. assists in maintaining an inventory of materials and equipment
k. assists with the repair of damaged materials and equipment
l. removes materials for school librarian review according to established procedures
m. downloads, duplicates, or records media as requested within copyright guidelines
n. assists with marketing of the school library, for example, preparation of bulletin boards, displays, flyers, and announcements
o. understands school library program policies and the privacy issues related to student and teacher utilization of resources

Table 4.4 School Library Paraprofessional Sample Evaluation Form

Name _____

School _____

Date _____

Evaluation Ratings:

 3   **Exceeds Expectation**
 2   **Meets Expectation**
 1   **Needs Improvement**
NA   **Not Applicable**

Table 4.4 School Library Paraprofessional Sample Evaluation Form (*Continued*)

Performance Area	Rating	Comments
1. Acquisition of new resources: Checks to see if resources are in collection, identifies vendors and prices, orders resources, checks resources when received, follows up on any problems, claims missing magazines		
2. Processing new resources and equipment: Stamps with ownership identification, adds call numbers, inputs information into online catalog		
3. Resource distribution: Circulates resources and equipment efficiently, overdue notices, returns resources to proper place in timely manner		
4. Assists students and teachers: Assists in finding and using resources and equipment, demonstrates use of equipment and software		
5. Supervises school library student assistants: Provides training, oversees their work, schedules times to work, brings any problems to attention of school librarian		
6. Bibliographies and reports: Done in timely manner; neat, accurate, furnished on request		
7. Record keeping: Kept current, done efficiently, presented in a readable form		
8. Inventory of resources and equipment: Assists in inventory, follows up on discrepancies, provides report of missing items		
9. Repair of resources and equipment: Identifies items needing repair, completes repairs in timely manner, arranges for equipment to be sent out for repair, keeps records of equipment repair		
10. Removal of materials for school librarian review: Follows established procedures, done in timely manner		
11. Downloads, duplicates, or records media within copyright guidelines Done when requested, can operate equipment		
12. Marketing: Makes attractive displays and bulletin boards, develops brochures when needed		
13. Personal qualities: Arrives at work on time, treats school library users with respect, is pleasant to be around, has initiative, can work without constant direct supervision		
14. Ethical Behavior: Follows school library privacy policies regarding circulation of resources		

School Library Technical Paraprofessional

Job Description
Suggested Duties and Responsibilities
Duties

a. sets up equipment and networks
b. supports LAN and WAN
c. troubleshoots hardware, software, and networks
d. assembles, installs, and upgrades hardware
e. installs and upgrades software
f. repairs and maintains technology hardware
g. schedules maintenance for technology hardware
h. offers technical advice on hardware and software
i. provides technical training and in-services to district staff
j. participates in continuing education as appropriate
k. assumes other duties as directed

Table 4.5 School Library Technical Paraprofessional Sample Evaluation Form

Name _____

School _____

Date _____

Evaluation Ratings:
  3 **Exceeds Expectation**
  2 **Meets Expectation**
  1 **Needs Improvement**
 NA **Not Applicable**

Performance Area	Ratings	Comments

1. Dets up equipment and networks:
   Done in timely manner, keeps classroom disruption to a
     minimum, consults with others when needed		

2. Supports LAN and WAN: Keeps networks working, knowledgeable about network		

3. Repair and maintenance of hardware and networks:
   Can troubleshoot problems, repairs done in a timely
     manner, performs routine maintenance on
     scheduled basis		

Table 4.5 School Library Technical Paraprofessional Sample Evaluation Form (*Continued*)

Performance Area	Ratings	Comments
4. Assembles, installs, and upgrades hardware: Has schedule of replacement, work completed in timely fashion, considers district tech plan and use of equipment, makes recommendations, researches upgrade needs		
5. Installs and upgrades software: Makes recommendations for upgrading, considers district tech plan and use of software, keeps classroom disruptions to a minimum		
6. Technical advice: Reads variety of appropriate journals, is knowledgeable about new trends, understands classroom use of equipment and software, makes suggestions and recommendations		
7. Training and in-service: Provided in timely manners, follows up on training, offers further assistance, communicates effectively with staff		
8. Personal qualities: Arrives at work on time, can communicate with staff in terms they understand, is cooperative, prioritizes work		

School Library Student Assistant

Job Description
Suggested Duties and Responsibilities
Duties

a. understands privacy issues related to student and teacher utilization of resources
b. assists the school librarian in providing high-quality services
c. assists with the processing of newly acquisitioned resources
d. circulates resources to school library users, using the electronic circulation system, if available
e. returns borrowed materials to their appropriate locations
f. assists with the mending of books and other materials
g. operates, maintains, and troubleshoots school library program equipment
h. helps school library users locate and retrieve information
i. creates displays and bulletin boards
j. participates in activities that promote the use and image of the school library
k. performs other routine tasks under the direction of the school librarian

Table 4.6 School Library Student Assistant Sample Evaluation Form

Name _____

School _____

Date _____

Evaluation Ratings:
- 3 **Exceeds Expectation**
- 2 **Meets Expectation**
- 1 **Needs Improvement**
- NA **Not Applicable**

1. Personal traits: Completes work on time, courteous and helpful to other students, reports on time, displays initiative, follows general school behavior rules		
2. Ethical Behavior: Follows school library privacy policies regarding circulation of resources		
3. Circulation Desk: Charges and discharges resources efficiently, knows procedure		
4. Shelving resources: Items reshelved in a timely manner, returned to proper place		
5. Digital resources: Knows how to use online catalog and other digital resources available through the school library program		
6. Print resources: Is able to retrieve resources, knows where resources are stored		
7. Delivers equipment to classroom: Done on time, checks schedule throughout the day, assists with scheduling use		
8. Displays and bulletin boards: Changed regularly, artistically done, promotes school library and reading		
9. Processing of new resources: Adheres to established procedures, work is neat and accurate		
10. Mending of resources: Demonstrates ability to repair damaged resources properly, completes task in a timely manner		
11. Troubleshooting equipment: Can assist school library user when problems arise, knows what should be checked first, knows when to relay problem to another person		

SUMMARY

In addition to providing materials and activities for students to develop skills in independent reading and lifelong learning, an effective school library program ensures that students learn to access and evaluate information and apply information technology effectively. The school librarian is responsible for administering the school library program as well as being a member of the school's instructional team. The school librarian collaborates with teachers to develop and implement information, media, and technology literacy skills across all areas of the curriculum. Support personnel for the school library program help ensure that the school librarian has time for planning, development, and implementation of educational library services for students and teachers.

REFERENCES

American Association of School Librarians. *Empowering Learners: Guidelines for School Library Media Programs*. Chicago: American Library Association, 2009.

Nebraska State Board of Education. 2009. *Rule 10 Regulations and Procedures for the Accreditation of Schools, Title 92, Nebraska Administrative Code, Chapter 10*. http://www.nde.state.ne.us/LEGAL/documents/Rule10July72009-clean.pdf.

ADDITIONAL READINGS

American Association of School Librarians. *AASL Standards for the 21st-Century Learner*. Chicago: American Library Association, 2007.

Helvering, Donna. 2005. "Indicators of Effective Information Specialists." Millard Public Schools, Omaha, Nebraska.

International Society for Technology in Education. *ISTE National Educational Technology Standards for Teachers*. 2nd ed. Eugene: ISTE, 2008. http://www.iste.org/Content/Navigation Menu/NETS/ForTeachers/2008Standards/.

"Iowa School Library Program Guidelines: Libraries, Literacy and Learning for the 21st Century." http://www.iowa.gov/educate/content/view/959/493/.

Woolls, Blanche. School *Library Media Manager*. 4th ed. Library and Information Science Text Series. Westport: Libraries Unlimited, 2008.

5

Teaching for Learning and the School Library Program

RATIONALE

Teaching for learning is the focus of an effective school library program. The school librarian teaches learners to use skills, resources, and tools to inquire, understand, and use information and knowledge for intellectual and personal growth. The school librarian develops a program that provides the environment and framework necessary for optimal teaching and learning. The leadership of the school librarian is the catalyst for successful collaborative teaching and learning in the school library program.

The focus of the school library program is to prepare students for a future rich in information, promoting technology as a tool and teaching ethical use of information and social responsibility. Programs must be student-centered, bringing together information, people, ideas, learning experiences, and technology. Within this framework, the school librarian promotes technology as a tool and teaches ethical use and social responsibility, thus preparing learners for an information-complex world.

RESOURCES

For students to become information literate and lifelong learners, they need a variety of diverse resources, both digital and print, that build skills, encourage inquiry, and offer multiple perspectives. The purpose of the school library program is to provide current technology to facilitate information access and organization and to showcase information products. The American Association of School Librarians (AASL 2007) *Standards for the 21st-Century Learner*, along with the AASL (2009a, 2009b) guidelines for implementation, *Empowering Learners: Guidelines for School Library Media Programs* and *AASL Standards for the 21st-Century Learner in Action*, and the International Society for Technology in Education's (ISTE 2007) *National Educational Technology Standards for Students* and its accompanying guidelines, *NETS for Teachers* (ISTE 2008), serve as a framework for teaching and learning in the school library program. The AASL and ISTE standards both complement the Partnership for 21st-Century Skills (P21).

MISSION STATEMENT

Every school librarian needs to develop a mission statement for the program based on the needs of the local community and school culture. Combined with the AASL mission statement, the local school library mission statement should guide the actions of the program. (See chapter 1 for more information related to developing a mission statement.)

AASL Mission of the School Library Program

The AASL mission statement for the school library program was revised in the 2009 *Empowering Learners: Program Guidelines for School Library Programs* and reads as follows:

The mission of the school library media program is to ensure that students and staff are effective users of ideas and information. The school librarian empowers students to be critical thinkers, enthusiastic readers, skillful researchers, and ethical users of information by:

- collaborating with educators and students to design and teach engaging learning experiences that meet individual needs.
- instructing students and assisting educators in using, evaluating, and producing information and ideas through active use of a broad range of appropriate tools, resources, and information technologies.
- providing access to materials in all formats, including up-to-date, high quality, varied literature to develop and strengthen a love of reading.
- providing students and staff with instruction and resources that reflect current information needs and anticipate changes in technology and education.
- providing leadership in the total education program and advocating for strong school library media programs as essential to meeting local, state, and national education goals (AASL 2008)

Excerpted from *Empowering Learners: Guidelines for School Library Programs*, by the American Association of School Librarians, a division of the American Library Association, copyright © 2009, American Library Association. Used with permission.

ROLES OF THE SCHOOL LIBRARIAN

In 2009, the role of the school librarian was defined in *Empowering Learners: Guidelines for School Library Media Programs* as that of a leader, teacher, instructional partner, information specialist, and program administrator (AASL 2009, 16). The school librarian draws on each of these roles in developing a library program that focuses on teaching for learning.

In 2006, the AASL Board of Directors brought together leading school library professionals from different locales, backgrounds, and experiences to define the role of the school librarian. Instructional partner was ranked number one, followed by information specialist, teacher, and program administrator. At that time, the fifth role was added, the role of leader. Participants felt that this addition completed the roles and was key to developing a successful school library program.

Defining the Roles of the School Librarian

Leader

As a leader, the school librarian envisions the exemplary school library program. This involves planning a program that meets the mission and goals of the school district and successfully articulating the plan to the school community. The school librarian serves as an instructional leader for curriculum, policy, staff development, and planning for emerging technologies. As a creative motivator, the school librarian develops an environment that draws students, staff, and administrators into the school library, making it the heart of the learning community. Professional responsibilities take the school librarian beyond the walls of the library to become a leader not only at the building level but also at the district, state, and national levels. As a leader, the school librarian is a passionate innovator, consensus builder, collaborator, professional learner, connector, advocate, visionary, and change agent.

Instructional Partner

To be a successful instructional partner, the school librarian needs to be a collaborator, becoming an indispensable member of the instructional team. By integrating the *AASL Standards for 21st-Century Learners*, the school librarian guides students in developing critical thinking skills, making informed decisions, using information ethically, and sharing information through creative and artistic means. The school librarian plays an active role in formative and summative assessment for students, thus becoming an integral partner with the classroom teacher in ensuring that students master instructional objectives. As an instructional partner, the school librarian is a collaborator, communicator, and architect of instructional design.

Information Specialist

It is the role of the school librarian to expand the learning community, creating a virtual global environment, a learning commons. To accomplish this requires expertise in identifying, evaluating, and acquiring information sources that leads to a balanced library collection that not only supports curriculum objectives but also meets the needs of all learners. Using technology as a tool to make resources accessible from and through the school library, the school librarian demonstrates how to access, evaluate, utilize, and archive information. The school librarian must teach and model the ethical use of information and social networking tools in a digital age and empower learners to become information producers as well as consumers. The information expertise of the school librarian positions him or her to be an invaluable resource to individuals within the learning community. As an information specialist, the school librarian is an information expert, scholar, evaluator, global thinker, and innovator.

Teacher

The school librarian is a teacher of information literacy, instructing students to acquire and use skills, resources, and tools and apply these skills to an inquiry process. In this role, the school librarian promotes reading as an essential skill, encouraging students to read for pleasure, understanding, and purpose while gaining the ability to construct new meaning. The school librarian promotes reading from a variety of formats, both digital and textual. It is important that students read materials that help them understand and appreciate global and multicultural perspectives. In the role of teacher, the school librarian guides students to identify and develop learning dispositions while helping students assess their learning. As a teacher, the school librarian is a motivator, researcher, lifelong learner, and active promoter of resources and learning.

Program Administrator

The school librarian oversees the needs and interests of the school learning community by developing a program and facility to empower the 21st-century learners and teachers. This would include using management skills to develop and implement a mission statement; strategic plan; policies, including copyright, intellectual freedom, and fair use issues; professional development; and budget. As program administrators, the school librarian is a collaborative partner, facilitator, entrepreneur, catalyst, and evaluator.

COLLABORATIVE PLANNING AND TEACHING

The collaborative planning and teaching process is essential to the teaching and learning component of the successful school library program. Collaborative planning allows the school librarian and the classroom teacher to design instruction that promotes effective teaching of information literacy skills, the inquiry process, and the use of resources and tools. In *Cognition, Teaching, and Assessment*, Michael Pressley and Christine McCormick (1995) identify the best practice for meaningful instruction of information literacy skills:

- embedded and relevant to student needs
- described and modeled
- teach students when, why, and where they can use strategies
- repeatedly practiced
- reinforced through feedback

The school librarian and classroom teacher act as partners to combine expertise and knowledge of information literacy skills, curriculum, technology, and standards to increase student achievement and prepare students for lifelong learning.

Collaborative planning is enhanced by the presence of the following essential elements:

- shared philosophy, vision, and goals
- mutual respect and trust
- flexibility and creativity

- open communication
- initial formal planning
- knowledge of
  - best practice and instructional design
  - curriculum and standards
  - information literacy
  - inquiry process
  - formative and summative assessment
- technology skills
- available resources and staffing
- unified approach to classroom management
- continuous reflective assessment, including documentation of successes and failures
- administrative support
- flexible scheduling of the school library
- staff development
- time management

Benefits of Collaborative Planning

Collaborative planning helps students do the following:

- participate in authentic inquiry
- increase achievement
- use information literacy skills and inquiry
- use resources optimally
- receive immediate assistance and reinforcement
- become effective users of information
- develop excitement for learning
- make learning and reading relevant
- experience varied learning and teaching styles
- enhance lifelong learning skills
- work in small groups or independently
- become collaborators
- use libraries independently
- use information ethically

Collaborative planning and teaching helps classroom teachers and the school librarian do the following:

- correlate information literacy skills and curriculum
- link learning, instruction, resources, and information literacy
- provide effective team instruction
- develop meaningful professional relationships
- learn from colleagues
- promote a positive learning climate
- optimize time, resources, skills, and talents
- provide a better student-teacher ratio

Collaborative planning and teaching helps administrators do the following:

- increase student achievement
- develop a cohesive instructional staff
- provide an appealing environment for the learning community
- ensure the acquisition of adequate and appropriate resources
- advocate for the integration of school library program goals and objectives
- recognize the role of the school librarian in student learning

Collaborative Planning Process Form

To help facilitate collaborative planning, a form is an effective tool for the school librarian and the classroom teacher as they plan instructional units to integrate information literacy skills and resources. This initial planning helps clarify objectives and roles and lets the teacher know that the school librarian understands good instructional practice and design and can act as an effective coteacher. A collaborative plan should include who, what, when, where, and how it will be done and should address assessment of student learning (see Figure 5.1).

INFORMATION LITERACY AND LEARNING STANDARDS

Various professional associations and initiatives (e.g., AASL, ISTE, P21) provide standards for essential learning for information literacy. The school librarian needs to consider and articulate to others how these standards relate to curriculum standards at the national, state, and local levels.

AASL Standards for the 21st-Century Learner

AASL has determined four major standards areas that are integral to the development of the 21st-century learner. Skills, actions, responsibilities, and self-assessment strategies are defined and described within each of the four major standards. A full listing of the standards and indicators can be accessed on the AASL Web site (http://www.ala.org/aasl/standards/). According to the AASL standards, learners use skills, resources, and tools to do the following:

1. inquire, think critically, and gain knowledge
2. draw conclusions, make informed decisions, apply knowledge to new situations, and create new knowledge

Figure 5.1 Collaborative Planning Guide

Teacher: Course: Project due date:	Teacher e-mail: Grade level: Class size: Dates in the school library:

Project Title and Description: *Develop central idea/theme and supporting concepts*

Curriculum Objectives:

Information Literacy Skills Objectives:

Research/Inquiry Model: *Such as Big6, Super3, 5-As, I-Search, the Research Cycle, other.*

AASL Standards for the 21st-Century Learner: (www.ala.org/aasl/standards) ☐ Inquire, think critically, and gain knowledge. ☐ Draw conclusions, make informed decisions, apply knowledge to new situations, and create new knowledge. ☐ Share knowledge and participate ethically and productively as members of our democratic society. ☐ Pursue personal and aesthetic growth. Excerpted from *Standards for the 21st-Century Learner*, by the American Association of School Librarians, a division of the American Library Association, copyright © 2007 American Library Association. Available for download at www.ala.org/aasl/standards. Used with permission.

End Product:

Resources: *Such as books, databases, Web sites, software, interviews*

RESEARCH TASKS

	School Librarian	Teacher
Facilitate development of guiding questions		
Create note-taking organizer (folder, graphic organizer)		
Consider possible research sources (textual and digital)		
Teach introductory content		
Teach research/inquiry/information literacy skills		
Teach technology skills		
Determine how student progress will be monitored		
Assess student growth		
Additional needs/tasks		

REFLECT AND EVALUATE *throughout the project*
What worked well?
What changes need to be made?
Additional information/comments:

3. share knowledge and participate ethically and productively as members of our democratic society

4. pursue personal and aesthetic growth (AASL 2009, 160)

Excerpted from *Standards for the 21st-Century Learner*, by the American Association of School Librarians, a division of the American Library Association, copyright © 2007, American Library Association. Available for download at http://www.ala.org/aasl/standards/. Used with permission.

2007 ISTE National Educational Technology Standards for Students

ISTE has identified six major standards areas that are integral to the development of digital and higher-order thinking skills. The standards with indicators can be found on the ISTE Web site (ISTE, n.d.). The ISTE major standards are as follows:

1. Creativity and Innovation Students demonstrate creative thinking, construct knowledge, and develop innovative products and processes using technology.

2. Communication and Collaboration

   a. Students use digital media and environments to communicate and work collaboratively, including at a distance, to support individual learning and contribute to the learning of others.

3. Research and Information Fluency

   a. Students apply digital tools to gather, evaluate, and use information.

4. Critical Thinking, Problem Solving, and Decision Making

   a. Students use critical thinking skills to plan and conduct research, manage projects, solve problems, and make informed decisions using appropriate digital tools and resources.

5. Digital Citizenship

   a. Students understand human, cultural, and societal issues related to technology and practice legal and ethical behavior.

6. Technology Operations and Concepts

   a. Students demonstrate a sound understanding of technology concepts, systems, and operations. (ISTE 2007)

Excerpted from *National Educational Technology Standards for Students*, 2nd ed., copyright © 2007, ISTE, http://www.iste.org/. National Educational Technology Standards for Students (NETS•S) is available for download at http://www.iste.org/Content/NavigationMenu/NETS/ForStudents/2007Standards/NETS_for_Students_2007.htm. All rights reserved.

2008 ISTE National Educational Technology Standards for Teachers

Effective teachers model and apply NETS•S as they design, implement, and assess learning experiences to engage students and improve learning; enrich professional practice; and provide positive models for students, colleagues, and the community. The standards with indicators can be found on the ISTE Web site (ISTE, n.d.). The ISTE standards state that all teachers should meet the following standards:

1. Facilitate and Inspire Student Learning and Creativity

    a. Teachers use their knowledge of subject matter, teaching and learning, and technology to facilitate experiences that advance student learning, creativity, and innovation in both face-to-face and virtual environments.

2. Design and Develop Digital-Age Learning Experiences and Assessments

    a. Teachers design, develop, and evaluate authentic learning experiences and assessment incorporating contemporary tools and resources to maximize content learning in context and develop the knowledge, skills, and attitudes identified in the NETS•S.

3. Model Digital-Age Work and Learning

    a. Teachers exhibit knowledge, skills, and work processes representative of an innovative professional in a global and digital society.

4. Promote and Model Digital Citizenship and Responsibility

    a. Teachers understand local and global societal issues and responsibilities in an evolving digital culture and exhibit legal and ethical behavior in their professional practices.

5. Engage in Professional Growth and Leadership

    a. Teachers continuously improve their professional practice, model lifelong learning, and exhibit leadership in their school and professional community by promoting and demonstrating the effective use of digital tools and resources. (ISTE 2008)

Excerpted from *National Educational Technology Standards for Teachers*, 2nd ed., copyright © 2008, ISTE, http://www.iste.org/. Available for download at http://www.iste.org/Content/NavigationMenu/NETS/ForTeachers/2008Standards/NETS_for_Teachers_2008.htm. All rights reserved.

PARTNERSHIPS FOR 21ST-CENTURY SKILLS

P21 is a national organization that advocates for 21st-century readiness for every student. Following is a brief overview of the P21 initiative. Many states have become P21 partners. A more in-depth overview of each section can be found on the P21 Web site (http://www.21stcenturyskills.org/index.php).

21st-Century Student Outcomes

The elements described in this section as "21st-century student outcomes" are the skills, knowledge, and expertise students should master to succeed in work and life in the 21st century.

1. core subjects and 21st-century themes
2. learning and innovation skills

   - creativity and innovation
   - critical thinking and problem solving
   - communication and collaboration

3. information, media, and technology skills

   - information literacy
   - media literacy
   - Information and Communications Technologies (ICT) literacy

4. life and career skills (Partnership for 21st Century Skills [P21] 2004)

21st-Century Support Systems

The elements described subsequently are the critical systems necessary to ensure student mastery of 21st-century skills. Twenty-first-century standards, assessments, curriculum, instruction, professional development, and learning environments must be aligned to produce a support system that produces 21st-century outcomes for today's students.

1. 21st-Century Standards
2. Assessment of 21st-Century Skills
3. 21st-Century Curriculum and Instruction
4. 21st-Century Professional Development
5. 21st-Century Learning Environments (P21 2004)

Nebraska Language Arts Standards

State standards can be used as a natural link to the *AASL Standards for the 21st-Century Learner,* NETS, and P21. The following is an example of Nebraska standards for language arts followed by a simple correlation chart showing the standards for AASL, NETS, and P21. The same may be done with other state standards.

K–12 Comprehensive Reading Standard

Students will learn and apply reading skills and strategies to comprehend text.

knowledge of print
phonological awareness.
word analysis
fluency
vocabulary
comprehension

K–12 Comprehensive Writing Standard

Students will learn and apply writing skills and strategies to communicate.

writing process
writing genres

K–12 Comprehensive Speaking and Listening Standard

Students will learn and apply speaking and listening skills and strategies to communicate.

speaking skills
listening skills
reciprocal communication

K–12 Comprehensive Multiple Literacies Standard

Students will identify, locate, and evaluate information multiple literacies. (Nebraska Department of Education 2009)

Core Standards Correlation Chart

It is important to view state standards in correlation with national standards such as AASL, ISTE, and initiatives such as P21 to ensure that information and literacy and technology standards are met. This correlation chart shown in Figure 5.2 uses Nebraska standards as an example. It is a tool that can be expanded and used to show the common threads and gaps that exist in various standards documents, resulting in raised awareness and more thorough coverage of competencies needed by students to be successful learners and workers.

Figure 5.2 Alignment of Core Standards from AASL, ISTE, and the State of Nebraska

*AASL Standard for the 21st-Century Learner	**ISTE National Educational Technology Standards for Students	Nebraska Language Arts Standards
1. Inquire, think critically, and gain knowledge.	3. Research and information fluency 4. Critical thinking, problem solving, and decision making	K–12 Comprehensive READING Standard K–12 Comprehensive MULTIPLE LITERACIES Standard
2. Draw conclusions, make informed decisions, apply knowledge to new situations, and create new knowledge.	1. Creativity and innovation 6. Technology operations and concepts	K–12 Comprehensive READING Standard K–12 Comprehensive WRITING Standard
3. Share knowledge and participate ethically and productively as members of our democratic society.	2. Communication and collaboration 5. Digital citizenship	K–12 Comprehensive SPEAKING/LISTENING Standard
4. Pursue personal and aesthetic growth.	1. Creativity and innovation	

* Excerpted from *Standards for the 21st-Century Learner,* by the American Association of School Librarians, a division of the American Library Association, copyright © 2007 American Library Association. Available for download at http://www.ala.org/aasl/standards. Used with permission.
** *National Educational Technology Standards for Students,* 2nd ed., copyright © 2007, International Society for Technology in Education, http://www.iste.org. NETS•S available for download at http://www.iste.org/Content/NavigationMenu/NETS/ForStudents/2007Standards/NETS_for_Students_2007.htm. All rights reserved.

CURRICULUM: TEACHING THE PROCESS

Inquiry Learning Models

Knowledge and application of an inquiry process is central to successful information literacy instruction. The inquiry process is represented in many information models. The school librarian needs to be familiar with a variety of models, choosing the one that best fits the objectives and instructional level of the learner. Further information about several models can be found on the Information Age Inquiry (2009) Web site under "Models."

The models listed here are representative of several process models available for implementation. It is not meant to be a comprehensive list. They are presented in alphabetical order.

Five As, Developed by Ian Jukes

Using words that begin with the letter *A*, students are guided to process information:

- Asking—key questions
- Accessing—relevant information
- Analyzing—information
- Applying—information to a task
- Assessing—the end results and the process (Jukes et al. 1998)

Big6™ and Super3™, Developed by Michael B. Eisenberg and Robert E. Berkowitz

One of the first of the current formal models for information processing, this system uses a problem-solving methodology (http://www.big6.com/).

Big6 Steps

- task definition
- information-seeking strategies
- location and access
- use of information
- synthesis
- evaluation (Eisenberg 2001)

Super3 Steps

- plan
- do
- review (Eisenberg 2001)

I-Search, Developed by Ken Macrorie, Marilyn Joyce, and Julie Tallman

This inquiry model emphasizes the interest of the student to develop a personal experience with the research process while encouraging writing skills. The four steps in this model are as follows:

- selecting a topic—based on interests, ideas, and resources
- finding information—questioning and exploring resources
- using information—note taking and analyzing information
- developing a final product—communicating findings and sharing the experience (Macrorie 1988)

Millard Research Model, Developed by Information Specialists of Millard Public Schools, Nebraska

Drawing from a variety of inquiry models, this system employs a seven-step approach to guiding students to internalize the research process:

- form questions
- plan research
- gather and record information
- organize information
- draw conclusions
- communicate information
- reflect and evaluate (Media and Information Services 2008)

Research Cycle, Developed by Jamie McKenzie

With a focus on students coming to their to own conclusions rather than reporting information that has been collected, the Research Cycle cycles allows students to inquire as they move through the research process (http://questioning.org/rcycle.html).
An explanation of the stages follows:

- Questioning: Identify questions then clarify the essential learning to take place.
- Planning: Determine the best places and ways to find and record relevant and reliable information.
- Gathering: Collect information that may be potentially useful and record the source(s).
- Sorting and Sifting: Systematically organize the information the may be used and lead to deeper understanding.
- Synthesizing: Arrange and rearrange the information into meaningful patterns for utilization.
- Evaluating: Determine what questions have yet to be answered, what remains to be asked, and what sources will provide additional information.

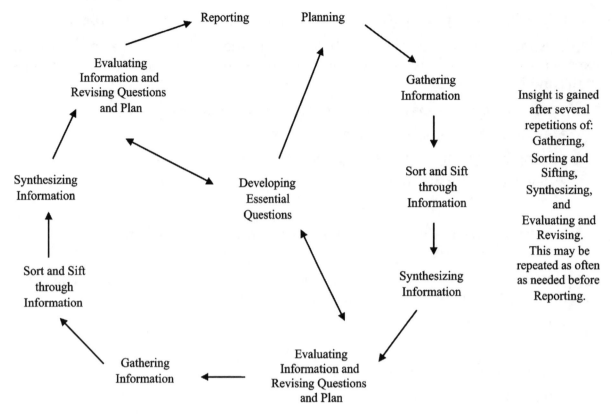

Figure 5.3 Research Cycle, Developed by Jamie McKenzie

Before reaching the final stage, repetitions through the previous stages help to expand and solidify what has been learned.

- Reporting: Determine the newly acquired insights to be shared and put them into an appropriate format. (McKenzie 1999, 2000)

The Stripling Model of Inquiry, Developed by Barbara K. Stripling

The Stripling Model of Inquiry is a six-phase model for the inquiry cycle of learning that encourages students to develop high-level thinking skills and critical analysis as they proceed through this research process. Elements of this model follow:

- connect
- wonder
- investigate
- construct
- express
- reflect (Stripling 2003)

ASSESSMENT OF STUDENT LEARNING AND LEARNING PROCESSES

Assessment is used to monitor and determine student achievement and the effectiveness of information literacy instruction. The school librarian develops and implements assessments that measure both formative and summative growth. A variety of assessments, both formal and informal, may be used. Students should learn self-assessment strategies as a tool for reflecting on their own academic and personal growth and demonstrate the dispositions of a competent learner. Self-assessment strategies and dispositions are outlined in the AASL (2009b) *AASL Standards for the 21st-Century Learner in Action.*

Formative and Summative

Formative assessments provide periodic measurement during the instructional sequence. Summative assessment measures student progress at the conclusion of a particular learning experience.

Assessment Examples

EXIT TICKET

This assessment allows the educator to measure specific student learning. For example, students may be asked to list six elements of good note taking. The list is turned in as students exit. It can be formal or informal.

RUBRIC

Rubrics, a form of summative assessment, are scoring guides in grid design. Rubrics should be used at the beginning of a project to state expectations and at the end to assess learning and performance. Students and teachers can easily determine the criteria for performance as ranked on the rubric. Examples and guides to develop rubrics can be found at *RubiStar* (U.S. Department of Education 2008).

CHECKLISTS

A checklist is a list of parameters and behaviors to be demonstrated during the course of an information literacy project. Students can use a checklist to assess progress throughout the project.

RETRIEVAL CHART

A retrieval chart is a note-taking chart. Periodic examination of the chart by the teacher can yield information about successful note taking and information collection. Guiding questions are listed at the top of a column with bulleted notes recorded under each question. This can be a form of formative and/or summative assessment.

PRE- AND POSTASSESSMENTS

Pre- and posttests are an effective demonstration of learning growth. *Trails* (Kent State University Libraries 2010) is an online example of an assessment for information literacy skills that can be used at the beginning and end of a unit. It can be accessed online at http://www.trails-9.org/.

REFERENCES

American Association of School Librarians. 2007. *Standards for the 21st-Century Learner.* http://www.ala.org/aasl/standards.

American Association of School Librarians. *Empowering Learners: Guidelines for School Library Media Programs.* Chicago: American Library Association, 2009a.

American Association of School Librarians. *AASL Standards for the 21st-Century Learner in Action.* Chicago: American Library Association, 2009b.

Eisenberg, Mike. 2001. "Big6™ Skills Overview." http://www.big6.com/2001/11/19/a-big6%e2%84%a2-skills-overview/.

Information Age Inquiry. 2009. "Models." http://www.virtualinquiry.com/inquiry/models.htm.

International Society for Technology in Education. *National Educational Technology Standards for Students.* Eugene: International Society for Technology in Education, 2007.

International Society for Technology in Education. *National Educational Technology Standards for Teachers.* Eugene: International Society for Technology in Education, 2008.

International Society for Technology in Education. n.d. *National Educational Technology Standards.* http://www.iste.org/AM/Template.cfm?Section=NETS/.

Jukes, Ian, et al. *NetSavvy: Information Literacy for the Communication Age.* International Society for Technology, 1999.

Kent State University Libraries. 2010. *TRAILS: Tool for Real-Time Assessment of Information Literacy Skills.* http://www.trails-9.org/.

Macrorie, Ken. *The I-Search Paper.* Portsmouth: Heinemann, 1988.

McKenzie, Jamie. 1999. "The Research Cycle, 2000." *FNO* 9, No. 4. http://questioning.org/rcycle.html.

McKenzie, Jamie. *Beyond Technology: Questioning Research and the Information Literate School.* Bellingham: FNO Press, 2000.

Media and Information Services. *The Millard Research Model.* Omaha: Millard Public Schools, 2008.

Nebraska Department of Education. *Nebraska Language Arts Standards.* Omaha: Nebraska Department of Education, 2009.

Partnership for 21st Century Skills. 2004. *A Framework for 21st Century Learning.* http://www.21stcenturyskills.org/.

Pressley, Michael, and Christine McCormick. *Cognition Teaching, and Assessment.* New York: HarperCollins, 1995.

Stripling, Barbara K. "Inquiry-Based Learning." In *Curriculum Connections through the Library: Principles and Practice*, ed. Barbara K. Stripling and Sandra Hughes-Hassell. Westport: Libraries Unlimited, 2003.

U.S. Department of Education. 2008. *RubiStar.* http://rubistar.4teachers.org/.

ADDITIONAL READING

Alley, Kathleen M. *Teaching Integrated Reading Strategies in the Middle School Library Media Center.* Westport: Libraries Unlimited, 2008.

Arter, Judith A. *Creating and Recognizing Quality Rubrics.* Portland: ETS, 2006.

Bailey, Alison L. *Formative Assessment for Literacy, Grades K–6: Building Reading and Academic Language Skills across the Curriculum.* Thousand Oaks: Corwin Press, 2008.

Bankhead, Elizabeth, Janet Nichols, and Dawn Vaughn. *Write It!* Santa Barbara: Libraries Unlimited, 2009.

Berger, Pam, and Sally Trexler. *Choosing Web2.0 Tools for Learning and Teaching in a Digital World.* Santa Barbara: Libraries Unlimited, 2010.

Blankstein, Alan M., Robert W. Cole, and Paul D. Houston, eds. *Engaging Every Learner.* Thousand Oaks: Corwin Press, 2007.

Boss, Suzie. *Reinventing Project-Based Learning: Your Field Guide to Real-World Projects in the Digital Age.* Eugene: International Society for Technology in Education, 2007.

Brookhart, Susan M. *How to Give Effective Feedback to Your Students.* Alexandria: Association for Supervision and Curriculum Development, 2008.

Buzzeo, Toni. *Collaborating to Meet Standards: Teacher/Librarian Partnerships for K–6.* Worthington: Linworth, 2007.

Callison, Daniel, and Leslie B. Preddy. *The Blue Book on Information Age Inquiry, Instruction and Literacy.* Westport: Libraries Unlimited, 2006.

Cavanaugh, Terence W., and Nancy J. Keane. *The Tech-Savvy Booktalker: A Guide for 21st-Century Educators.* Westport: Libraries Unlimited, 2008.

Conroy, Helen, and Jo Webb. *A Guide to Teaching Information Literacy.* New York: Neal-Schuman, 2009.

Courtney, Nancy D. *Library 2.0 and Beyond: Innovative Technologies and Tomorrow's User.* Westport: Libraries Unlimited, 2007.

Crane, Beverley E. *Using Web 2.0 Tools in the K–12 Classroom.* New York: Neal-Schuman, 2009.

Donham, Jean. *Enhancing Teaching and Learning.* 2nd ed. New York: Neal-Schuman, 2008.

Dvetkovic, Vibiana Bowman, and Robert J. Lackie. *Teaching Generation M.* New York: Neal-Schuman, 2009.

Erkens, Cassandra, Chris Jakicic, Lillie G. Jessie, Dennis King, Sharon V. Kramer, Thomas W. Many, Mary Ann Ranells, Ainsley B. Rose, Susan K. Sparks, and Eric Twadell. *The

Collaborative Teacher: Working Together as a Professional Learning Community. Bloomington: Solution Tree, 2008.

Farmer, Leslie. *Your School Library: Check It Out!* Santa Barbara: Libraries Unlimited, 2009.

Fisher, Douglas. *Checking for Understanding: Formative Assessment Techniques for Your Classroom.* Bloomington: Association for Supervision and Curriculum Development, 2007.

Fontichiaro, Kristina. *21st-Century Learning in School Libraries.* Santa Barbara: Libraries Unlimited, 2009.

Frey, Nancy, and Douglas B. Fisher. *Teaching Visual Literacy: Using Comic Books, Graphic Novels, Anime, Cartoons, and More to Develop Comprehension and Thinking Skills.* Thousand Oaks: Corwin Press, 2008.

Garvin, Susan L. *A Is for Almanac: Complete Lessons to Teach the Uses of Reference Sources in Grades K–6.* New York: Neal-Schuman, 2008.

Gilmore, Barry. *Plagiarism: Why It Happens, How to Prevent It.* Portsmouth: Heinemann, 2008.

Godwin, Peter. *Information Literacy Meets Library 2.0.* New York: Neal-Schuman, 2008.

Griffin-Wiesner, Jennifer. *Teaching Kids to Change the World: Lessons to Inspire Social Responsibility for Grades 6–12.* Minneapolis: Search Institute Press, 2008.

Harada, Violet H. *Collaborating for Project-Based Learning in Grades 9–12.* Columbus: Linworth, 2008.

Harada, Violet H., and Joan M. Yoshina. *Assessing Learning: Librarians and Teachers as Partners.* Westport: Libraries Unlimited, 2005.

Harker, Christa. *Library Research with Emergent Reading: Meeting Standards through Collaboration.* Worthington: Linworth, 2008.

Ivers, Karen. *A Teacher's Guide to Using Technology in the Classroom.* Westport: Libraries Unlimited, 2009.

Jackson, Brooks. *Unspun: Finding Facts in a World of Disinformation.* New York: Random House Trade Paperbacks, 2007.

Janet, Murray R. *Achieving Educational Standards Using the Big6.* Columbus: Linworth, 2008.

Johnson, Mary J. *Primary Source Teaching the Web 2.0 Way, K–12.* Santa Barbara: Linworth, 2010.

Johnson, Peggy. *Fundamentals of Collection Development and Management.* Chicago: American Library Association, 2009.

Jones, Jami Biles. *The Power of Media Specialists to Improve Academic Achievement and Strengthen At-Risk Students.* Columbus: Linworth, 2008.

Jukes, Ian. *NetSavvy: Building Information Literacy in the Classroom.* Thousand Oaks: Corwin Press, 2000.

Kingore, Bertie W. *Developing Portfolios for Authentic Assessment, PreK–3: Guiding Potential in Young Learners.* Thousand Oaks: Corwin Press, 2008.

Knodt, Jean Sausele. *Nine Thousand Straws: Teaching Thinking through Open-Inquiry Learning.* Santa Barbara: Libraries Unlimited, 2008.

Knowles, Liz. *Differentiating Reading Instruction through Children's Literature.* Santa Barbara: Libraries Unlimited, 2009.

Koechlin, Carol. *Q Tasks: How to Empower Students to Ask Questions and Care about Answers.* Markham: Stenhouse, 2006.

Kuhlthau, Carol C., Leslie K. Maniotes, and Ann K. Caspari. *Guided Inquiry: Learning in the 21st Century.* Westport: Libraries Unlimited, 2007.

Lamb, Annette, and Daniel Callison. *Graphic Inquiry.* Santa Barbara: Libraries Unlimited, forthcoming.

Loertscher, David V. *The New Learning Commons Where Learners Win! Reinventing School Libraries and Computer Labs.* Salt Lake City: Hi-Willow, 2008.

Lupa, Robyn M. *More Than MySpace: Teen, Librarians, and Social Networking.* Santa Barbara: Libraries Unlimited, 2009.

Mackey, Thomas P., and Trudi F. Jacobson, eds. *Using Technology to Teach Information Literacy.* New York: Neal-Schuman, 2008.

Marzano, Robert J. *The Art and Science of Teaching: A Comprehensive Framework for Effective Instruction.* Alexandria: Association for Supervision and Curriculum Development, 2007.

Morgan, Norah. *Asking Better Questions.* Markham: Pembroke, 2006.

Mueller, Jon. *Assessing Critical Skills.* Worthington: Linworth, 2008.

Murray, Janet R. *Achieving Educational Standards Using the Big6.* Columbus: Linworth, 2008.

Nicholaus, Bret. *KidChat: 222 Creative Questions to Spark Conversations.* New York: Roaring Brook Press, 2004.

Nicholaus, Bret. *KidChat Gone Wild!* New York: Roaring Brook Press, 2007.

Nichols, Beverly, Gene Johnson, Kevin Singer, and Sue Shidaker. *Managing Curriculum and Assessment: A Practitioner's Guide.* Worthington: Linworth, 2006.

Olness, Rebecca. *Using Literature to Enhance Content Area Instruction: A Guide for K–5 Teachers.* Newark: International Reading Association, 2007.

Peters, Laurence. *Global Education: Using Technology to Bring the World to Your Students.* Eugene: International Society for Technology in Education, 2009.

Phillips, Susan P. *Great Displays for Your Library Step by Step.* Jefferson: McFarland, 2008.

Preddy, Leslie. *Social Readers: Promoting Reading in the 21st Century.* Santa Barbara: Libraries Unlimited, 2010.

Richardson, Will. *Blogs, Wikis, Podcasts, and Other Powerful Web Tools for Classrooms.* Thousand Oaks: Corwin Press, 2006.

Scales, Pat R. *Protecting Intellectual Freedom in Your School Library: Scenarios from the Front Lines.* Chicago: American Library Association, 2009.

Snyder, Judith. *Jump-Start Your Library: Hands-On Materials for Library Learning—Level A, Beginner.* Janesville: Upstart Books, 2008.

Snyder, Judith. *Jump-Start Your Library: Hands-On Materials for Library Learning—Level B, Intermediate and Level C, Advanced.* Fort Atkinson: Upstart Books, 2008.

Stiggins, Rick, Judith A. Arter, Jan Chappius, and Stephen Chappius, for ETS. *Classroom Assessment for Student Learning: Doing It Right—Using It Well.* Prentice Hall, 2007.

Stripling, Barbara K. *Curriculum Connections through the Library.* Westport: Libraries Unlimited, 2003.

Taylor, Joie. *Information Literacy and the School Library Media Center.* Westport: Libraries Unlimited, 2005.

Trilling, Bernie. *21st Century Skills: Learning for Life in Our Times.* San Francisco: Jossey-Bass, 2009.

Vance, Anita L., ed., and Robbie Nickel, assist. ed. *Assessing Student Learning in the School Library Media Center.* Chicago: ALA Editions, 2007.

Zmuda, Allison, and Violet Harad. *Librarians as Learning Specialists: Meeting the Learning Imperative for the 21st Century.* Westport: Libraries Unlimited, 2008.

6

Collection Development: Managing School Library Resources

RATIONALE

Collection development is the process by which the school library program collection is built, maintained, and updated. It incorporates activities such as inventory, purchasing new materials, and budgeting. Updating the collection is an important aspect of collection development. This includes the selection of new material and the weeding of material that is no longer appropriate for the collection.

The purpose of this chapter is to guide the school librarian through the process of developing an up-to-date and relevant collection based on a localized collection development plan. It will also provide guidance in the assessment and evaluation of the collection. As a result of this effort, future plans can be developed based on knowledge of current holdings and needs. A current collection reflects materials in a variety of formats, including print, nonprint, and digital information as well as the equipment needed to manage, produce, and use them. Each school library should have a local collection development plan that is based on a district selection policy. Instructional resources, in turn, should assist educators and students in meeting educational objectives.

FORMULATING A PLAN FOR COLLECTION DEVELOPMENT

School librarians should develop and follow a collection development plan to ensure a balanced, relevant, and comprehensive collection of materials that meet the needs of students, staff, and the curriculum. According to Bishop (2007, 9), a collection development plan reflects the following interdependent components:

- Becoming knowledgeable about the existing collection;
- Becoming familiar with the school and community;
- Assessing the needs of the school's curriculum and other programs;

- Assessing the specific needs of the users;
- Establishing collection development policies and procedures;
- Identifying criteria for selection of materials;
- Planning for and implementing the selection process;
- Acquiring and processing materials;
- Participating in resource sharing;
- Maintaining and preserving the collection;
- Providing physical and intellectual access to materials;
- Evaluating the collection.

Excerpted from *The Collection Program in Schools: Concepts, Practices, and Information Sources*, 4th ed., by Kay Bishop, copyright © 2007. Reproduced with permission of ABC-CLIO, LLC.

The American Association of School Librarians (AASL; 2009) publication *Empowering Learners: Guidelines for School Library Media Programs* can provide direction for collection development in the school library. In *Empowering Learners*, AASL's guidelines for collection and information access state that the library "includes a well-developed collection of books, periodicals, and nonprint material in a variety of formats that support curricular topics and are suited to inquiry learning and users' needs and interests" (AASL 2009, 38–39). The actions associated with this guideline include the following:

- collaborating with the teaching staff to develop an up-to-date collection of print and digital resources in multiple genres that appeals to differences in age, gender, ethnicity, reading abilities, and information needs
- advocating for and protecting intellectual access to information and ideas
- mapping the collection to ensure that it meets the needs of the school curriculum
- regularly seeking input from students through such tools as surveys and suggestion boxes to determine students' reading interests and motivations
- ensuring that the collection is centralized and decentralized as needed to support classroom activities and other learning initiatives in the school
- promoting alternative reading options through reading lists, bibliographies, and webliographies that include periodicals, best-seller lists, graphic novels, books, and Web sites in multiple languages
- linking the digital library to local, regional, or state online networks and connecting with other public or academic libraries to take advantage of available virtual resources to support the school curriculum
- tracking inventory in the school library media center, taking advantage of up-to-date automation systems, and keeping current with software releases and training
- conducting regular weeding to ensure that the library collection is up to date
- reviewing challenged materials using the reconsideration policy

Adapted from *Empowering Learners: Guidelines for School Library Media Programs*, by the American Association of School Librarians, a division of the American Library Association, copyright © 2009, American Library Association. Used with permission.

ELEMENTS OF COLLECTION DEVELOPMENT

- Examine the patron population: what are their ages, reading levels, interest areas, special needs groups (e.g., English as second language, visually impaired, preschool, gifted, special education), nonprint needs, and any additional information about the school population that may influence the collection?

- Examine curricular needs, including access to multiple learning formats for a variety of student learning styles and infusion of multicultural and nonbiased materials.

- Evaluate the collection in terms of the following:

  - content/validity
  - currency
  - condition
  - circulation
  - nonprint availability

- Use the collection evaluation to weed out materials that are obsolete, in poor repair, unused, inaccurate, biased, or in unusable formats.

- Develop an acquisition plan for the addition of new materials, updating obsolete sections, filling in gaps, and developing a balanced collection.

LIBRARY MATERIALS SELECTION POLICY

The school librarian needs to ensure that there is an approved selection policy for the school library program that it is updated regularly. If there is no policy, the school librarian should take the lead in creating a selection policy. According to *Empowering Learners* (AASL 2009, 37), "the school library media program includes policies, procedures, and guidelines that support equitable access to ideas and information throughout the school community." Position statements for the school library program, developed by AASL, may further assist the school librarian in the development of policy statements. These position statements may be found on the AASL (2010) Web site (http://www.ala.org/ala/mgrps/divs/aasl/aaslissues/positionstatements/position statements.cfm).

Another useful resource for developing a selection policy, the *Workbook for Selection Policy Writing*, is made available through the American Library Association (ALA; 2010) Office of Intellectual Freedom. This is a basic guide to why a selection policy is important, how to draft a policy, tools for building a collection, and procedures for responding to a challenge. The workbook is available online (http://www.ala.org/ala/issuesadvocacy/banned/challengeslibrarymaterials/essentialpreparation/work bookslctn/index.cfm and http://www.ala.org/ala/aboutala/offices/oif/challenge support/dealing/workbook.pdf).

Statement of Philosophy

This is a brief statement of the values and beliefs established for the school library program and how the resources in the library support and enrich the educational program of the school district. Materials from all available media forms are selected on the basis of interest, vocabulary, maturity, and ability levels of the students as well as the curricular and personal needs of the students.

Responsibility for Selection of Materials

The board of education, as the policy-making and governing body of the school district, is legally responsible for the selection and approval of all print and nonprint materials. However, selection of materials involves many people—administrators, teachers, coordinators, school librarians, and students. The responsibility for coordinating the selection of school library materials and making recommendations for purchase is delegated to the professionally trained school librarian.

Objectives of Selection

Material selection requires careful consideration of the objectives of the school library program. Consider the following objectives:

- to provide materials that will support, supplement, and enrich the curriculum, taking into consideration the varied interests, abilities, and maturity levels of the faculty and students served
- to provide materials that will stimulate growth in factual knowledge, literary appreciation, aesthetic values, and ethical standards
- to stimulate a love of reading, viewing, listening, and learning that will provide for recreation and personal enjoyment and will encourage a continuing self-education, enabling the ability to make intelligent judgments in daily life
- to provide materials representative of the many religious, ethnic, and cultural groups
- to provide materials on opposing sides of controversial issues so that young citizens may develop skills in critical analysis and to learn to make informed decisions
- to place principles above personal opinion and reason above prejudice in the selection of materials of the highest quality to ensure a comprehensive collection appropriate for the users of the library
- to provide an understanding of American freedoms and a desire to preserve these freedoms through the development of informed and responsible citizenship

Selection Criteria

Materials are considered on the basis of the following:

- overall purpose
- timeliness or permanence

- potential use
- importance of the subject matter
- quality of the writing/production
- readability and popular appeal
- authoritativeness
- reputation and significance of the author, artist, composer, or producer
- format and price

Selection and evaluation should be a systematic, continuous process throughout the year so that school library resources will be balanced in terms of both curriculum needs and the needs and interests of individual students and instructors. Materials that are outdated or damaged should be removed and replaced, if appropriate. Requests from faculty and students are encouraged. Selection should be based on the needs of all school personnel and students. The departments in which the most use will occur should evaluate materials, if possible. Gift materials are judged by basic selection standards and are accepted or rejected by these standards.

Selection of Sensitive Material

Human sexuality: Authoritative information on this subject at the maturity level of the student should be included in the collection.

Language: Materials containing sexual terminology or profanity should not automatically be disqualified for library purchase, but they should meet a test of merit and suitability. (Ethnic literature often presents a set of values and a standard of language that are foreign to students. However, as students need to be helped to understand the people of different cultures, many of these books are considered suitable in meeting the test of merit that makes their purchase necessary.)

Religion: Factual and unbiased materials concerning major religions are acceptable. Sacred texts and historical matter are also acceptable, but other materials that expound sectarian beliefs shall be included only if there exists a well-defined instructional purpose for doing so. Periodicals published by religious bodies may be included for general news value if indexed in *Reader's Guide*, *Education Index*, or *Current Index to Journals in Education*.

Ideologies: Factual information on ideologies or philosophies that influence government, current events, politics, or education shall be acceptable.

Aids to Selection

Because no individual in a school system can read or view all materials, outside resources such as standard catalogs, book and audiovisual reviews, professional journals, and recommended book lists from professional organizations will be used. The following tools are recommended:

Children's Catalog, Wilson
Middle and Junior High School Library Catalog, Wilson
Senior High School Library Catalog, Wilson
Horn Book Guide and Horn Book Guide Online, Horn Book

Booklist and Booklist Online, ALA

Bulletin of the Center for Children's Books, University of Illinois

Horn Book Magazine, Horn Book

Multicultural Review, Goldman Group

School Library Journal, Reed Business Information

VOYA, Scarecrow Press

ALA/ALSC Book/Media Awards (*Newbery, Caldecott, Coretta Scott King, Pura Belpré, Theodor Seuss Geisel, Robert F. Sibert, Schneider Family, Michael L. Printz, and Notable Books* lists), http://www.ala.org/ala/mgrps/divs/alsc/awardsgrants/bookmedia/index.cfm

ALA/YALSA Best Books for Young Adults, http://www.ala.org/yalsa/booklists/

Notable Books for a Global Society, Children's Literature and Reading Special Interest Group of the International Reading Association, http://www.tcnj.edu/~childlit/index.htm (current), http://www.csulb.edu/org/childrens-lit/proj/nbgs/intro-nbgs.html (archived lists)

Notable Children's Books in the Language Arts, National Council of Teachers of English, http://childrensliteratureassembly.org/index.htm

Notable Trade Books for Young People, National Council for the Social Studies, http://www.socialstudies.org/notable/

Outstanding Science Trade Books for Students K–12, National Science Teachers Association, http://www.nsta.org/publications/ostb/

Children's Choices, International Reading Association, http://www.reading.org/resources/Booklists/ChildrensChoices.aspx

Young Adults' Choices, International Reading Association, http://www.reading.org/resources/Booklists/YoungAdultsChoices.aspx

Teachers' Choices, International Reading Association, http://www.reading.org/resources/Booklists/TeachersChoices.aspx

Orbis Pictus Award for Outstanding Nonfiction for Children, National Council of Teachers of English, http://www.ncte.org/awards/orbispictus/

Controversial Materials

There should be a section in the selection policy that deals with intellectual freedom and the handling of controversial materials. Most school districts have written policies that address this topic not only with regard to materials present in the school library but also for books or other formats used in classroom lessons. Thus it is important to include in the selection policy any school district policies that relate to controversial materials in a school library. This can be done in the text of the selection policy, or the school district policy can be placed in an appendix and referred to from the text.

Bishop (2007) advises that a statement that the school library supports the principle of intellectual freedom needs to be included and maintained and should include a statement of importance. Refer to the First Amendment to the U.S. Constitution or to other documents that address intellectual freedom in this section. The wording might read as follows: "The Lincoln School Library supports the principles of intellectual freedom inherent in the First Amendment to the [U.S. Constitution] as expressed in official statements of professional associations. These include [identify statement(s)] and form a part of this policy" (Bishop 2007, 45).

Excerpted from *The Collection Program in Schools: Concepts, Practices, and Information Sources*, 4th ed., by Kay Bishop, copyright © 2007. Reproduced with permission of ABC-CLIO, LLC.

Request for Reconsideration of Materials

Most selection policies also include procedures for handling complaints and focus complainant's attention on the principles of intellectual freedom rather than on the material itself. A school district may have specific procedures for dealing with challenged materials. In such a case, the school librarian will need to place these procedures in the library's policies and procedures document and make certain they are implemented correctly. If the steps to follow for challenged materials are not specified by the school district, then the school librarian should meet with an advisory board at school, develop the procedures, and put them through an approval process. Bishop lists the following possible steps to consider in a reconsideration of materials in the school library:

1. Listen calmly and with courtesy to the complainant.
2. Explain to the complainant the selection criteria used for materials that are in the media center and try to resolve the issue informally by discussing the educational uses of the material in question and noting relevant sections of the American Library Association's *Access to Resources and Services in the School Library Program: An Interpretation of the Library Bill of Rights*.
3. If the complainant wants to proceed with a formal request for reconsideration of a material, provide a copy of the policies and procedures related to the handling of challenged materials, as well as a copy of the school's *Request for Reconsideration of Library Resources* form.
4. Instruct the complainant that the form must be completed before a formal complaint proceeds.
5. Inform the principal of the challenge and the identity of the complainant (if the complaint is resolved informally, keep the identity of the complainant confidential).
6. When the complainant returns the completed form, the principal will inform the superintendent of schools of a request for formal reconsideration.
7. Form a reconsideration committee to include a building administrator, a classroom teacher from the appropriate grade level or subject area, the school library media specialist, an objective member of the community, and a student (if the challenged material is in a secondary school).
8. Appoint a chairperson for the committee.
9. Have the chairperson arrange a meeting of the committee to be held within ten working days after the form is returned to the school by the complainant.
10. At the first meeting, instruct all members of the committee to read the completed *Request for Reconsideration of Library Resources* form and to read, view, or listen to the material in question. The media specialist may need to obtain additional copies of the resource (book, video, or audiocassette) through

interlibrary loan or through informal means before a time for the next meeting can be set.

11. At a second meeting, when all committee members have had ample opportunity to examine and evaluate the challenged resource, discuss the material that has been questioned.

12. Instruct the committee members to form opinions on the resource as a whole, not on specific passages or selections.

13. Have the committee reach a decision, using majority rules, to retain or remove the item.

14. Have the chairperson complete a report of the committee's procedures and their decision regarding the challenged material and submit the report to the principal.

15. Instruct the principal to send a copy of the report to the complainant and discuss it with the complainant if so requested. Remind the principal to also submit a copy of the report to the superintendent of schools.

16. If the complainant continues to be dissatisfied with the process, inform that person that he or she has the right to appeal the decision of the committee to the superintendent of schools and the district school board.

17. Keep challenged materials in circulation until the process is complete. (Bishop 2007, 46–47)

Excerpted from *The Collection Program in Schools: Concepts, Practices, and Information Sources*, 4th ed., by Kay Bishop, copyright © 2007. Reproduced with permission of ABC-CLIO, LLC.

Collection Evaluation

To assist school librarians in evaluating the school library collection, it is important to gather information on how students, teachers, and administrators use the materials. "Some evaluation techniques that involve users include examining circulation statistics, determining the in-house use of materials, and conducting surveys. Collection-centered techniques, such as directly examining the collection and comparing their materials to lists or bibliographies, can also be used to evaluate a collection" (Bishop 2007, 15). Collection mapping is a form of evaluation that provides a way to determine the quantity and quality of the materials available in the school library, which shows exactly what materials are available for users.

Updating the Collection (Weeding)

To assist with improving the collection and to help alleviate misunderstandings about removal of items, it is a good idea to have a section in the school district's board-approved collection development policy that discusses the specifics of weeding (Baumbach and Miller 2006; Bishop 2007; Kerby 2006). This statement need not be complicated but should address the following: the person responsible for weeding, criteria, procedures, and disposal of removed items. If such a policy does not exist, you can find many helpful resources on the Internet to assist you in writing it (see "Additional Readings" at the conclusion of this chapter).

Table 6.1 General Evaluation of School Library Collection Management

School librarians may use the following rubric to evaluate the overall quality of the school library collection development process and to assist in planning sessions with school administrators.

0=Nonexistent   1=Poor   2=Fair   3=Good   4=Excellent

Criteria	0	1	2	3	4
1. The school library collection is selected and developed cooperatively by the certified school librarian and the faculty to support the school curriculum and to contribute to the learning goals of teachers and students, utilizing professional review publications and Web sites for selection of new resources.					
2. The school library collection includes resources in a variety of formats and reading levels with appropriate equipment selected to meet the learning needs of all students.					
3. Information services provide resources from outside the school library through interlibrary loan and electronic means to extend and expand the local collection.					
4. The school district has a written selection policy that has been approved by the school board and includes criteria and procedures for the selection, withdrawing, and reconsideration of resources.					
5. Each school building has its own collection development plan that supplements a district selection policy and provides specific guidelines for developing the school library collection.					
6. School library resources are selected according to principles of intellectual freedom and provide students with access to information that represents diverse points of view in a pluralistic society.					
7. All school library materials are included in a local public access catalog and standardized formats for classification and cataloging are followed.					
8. Collections and equipment are circulated according to procedures that ensure confidentiality of borrower records and promote free and easy access for all students and teachers.					
9. Access to information outside the school library is provided through other library resource collections and community resources through union catalogs, network arrangements, and resource sharing options.					
10. The school library collection is inventoried and evaluated on a continuing basis according to the guidelines in the selection policy.					

Adapted with permission of the American Association of School Librarians, a division of the American Library Association.

Table 6.2 School Library Materials and Equipment Inventory

School librarians may use this form when quantitatively evaluating the resources in the school library collection.

Media Type	Retrievable through the School Library	Available in District... (Specify Location)	Interlibrary Loan	Online Resource (Specify URL)
Resources:				
1. Hardback Books				
2. Paperback Books				
3. Books with Digital Formats				
4. Encyclopedias				
5. Magazines				
6. Newspapers				
7. Audiocassettes				
8. DVDs/Videocassettes				
9. CD-ROMs				
10. Computer Software				
11. Site Licenses				
12. Multimedia Kits				
13. Subscription Databases				
14. Tactile Formats (Models, Specimens, Sculptures, etc.)				
15. Graphics (Art Prints, Posters)				
16. Maps and Charts				
17. Other				
Professional Resources:				
1. Books				
2. Journals				
3. Computer Software				
4. Digital Formats (CD-ROMs, DVDs, eBooks, etc.)				
5. Other				
Equipment:				
1. Desktop Computers				
2. Laptop Computers				
3. Mouses				

Table 6.2 School Library Materials and Equipment Inventory (*Continued*)

Media Type	Retrievable through the School Library	Available in District . . . (Specify Location)	Interlibrary Loan	Online Resource (Specify URL)
4. Printers				
5. Barcode Readers				
6. Other Peripherals				
7. Computer/Equipment Carts				
8. Video Projectors				
9. Overhead Projectors				
10. LCD Projectors				
11. White Boards				
12. Screens				
13. Scanners				
14. Digital Cameras				
15. Video Cameras				
16. Digital Video Recorders				
17. VCR/DVD Players				
18. Television Monitors				
19. Tripods				
20. Tape Recorders				
21. Compact Disc Players				
22. High-Speed Duplicators				
23. Microphones				
24. Radios				
25. Mixers				
26. Closed-Circuit TV System				
27. Distance Learning Lab Equipment				
28. Film and Video Production Equipment				
29. Cable System				
30. Satellite				
31. Other				
32. FAX Machines				
33. Photocopy Machines				
34. Laminating Machines				
35. Paper Cutters				
36. Other				

The time designated for weeding the school library collection can occur in a variety of ways, to be determined by the school librarian. Continuous weeding involves constant identification of potential materials for evaluation on a day-to-day basis. Intermittent weeding targets specific sections of the collection for evaluation at different times during the school year. This weeding schedule also contains ways to enlist the aid of classroom teachers who know the curriculum and can offer information about materials in specific subject areas. Entire collection weeding allocates a block of time to weed the collection when the center is not in use.

The following questions may be useful in determining the criteria for evaluating the collection:

- *Content/validity:* Does the material support the curriculum? Is it free of biased or stereotypical portrayals? Is it accurate? Is it well written? Is the reading level appropriate?

- *Currency:* What is the copyright date? Is the information outdated? Is the topic no longer of interest to users?

- *Condition:* Is the material damaged? Are book pages torn, brittle, dirty, or missing? Is the binding in good shape? Has the book been repaired in the past? Does it have an uninviting appearance? Are nonprint materials scratched, torn, or faded?

- *Circulation:* When was the last checkout? How often has the book circulated? Is it used in-house? Are duplicate copies available? Is it available in another format? Is the hardware needed for nonprint material still available and in good operating condition? Does the item provide access to information that supports different learning styles?

Certain areas become obvious in their need for attention in the weeding process. Check the collection for the following possible weeds:

- yearbooks, almanacs, and directories

- materials older than 10 years in areas of philosophy; psychology; religion; language; social studies, including geography of the world; political science; commerce; and travel

- materials older than 5 years in all areas of pure science (with the exception of botany and natural history); applied science, including math; computers; photography, inventions, and careers; maps and globes; and encyclopedia sets

- history as told from a single perspective

Caution is required before weeding certain materials. Carefully consider before removing the following:

- newer materials that could benefit from promotion to improve circulation

- award winners and classics (unless newer editions are available)

- materials with a local focus (community and state history)

- school publications such as newspapers and yearbooks
- unabridged dictionaries
- art collections
- materials that help provide balance to the collection

Disposal Procedures

When it has been determined which materials are to be eliminated from the collection, employ steps for disposal, which may include the following:

- removal of records for each item from the circulation/catalog system
- removal of school identification markings and an indication of "DISCARD" on the items
- removal of materials from the school library by a method consistent with the collection development policy

BUDGETING

Funding must be available to keep the school library current. The budget must support the mission of the library and the school improvement plan. The school librarian needs to prepare a school library budget to ensure input in budget decisions and to avoid inconsistent patterns of acquisition that could result in an ineffective school library collection due to duplication of content, irrelevancy to the curriculum, student and teacher needs, or failure to provide user-centered information and resources. The school librarian should be involved in the budget planning process by providing budgetary information to school administrators so that funds will be available for developing an effective, balanced, and useful school library collection.

WEB SITE EVALUATION

Twenty-first-century learners need to develop the ability to use technology as a tool for gathering information now and in the future. The AASL (2007) *Standards for the 21st-Century Learner* address this need by identifying skills that call for *evaluation* of information in *all* formats through Standards 1.1.4, 1.1.5, 1.1.6, 1.1.7, and 1.24, 2.14. Print materials are evaluated before purchase, using the resources available, as part of the selection process. However, students are using the Internet more than ever for their information needs. Because no school librarian can possibly preview every Web site a student might access, evaluation skills need to be incorporated into information literacy instruction.

The following questions may guide students, teachers, and school librarians in evaluating Web sites:

- *Content:* What is the purpose of the Web site? Who is the intended audience? Is the content presented objectively? Does it support the curriculum?
- *Accuracy and Reliability:* When was the Web site last updated? Is the content original? Are the links up-to-date? Does it contain primary source material?

Table 6.3 School Library Program Budget

	One Year Preceding Current Year	Current Year	Projected Upcoming Year
Funding Sources:			
Local			
State			
Federal			
Other (Specify)			
Expenditures:			
1. Books:			
Hardback			
Paperback			
Encyclopedias/Reference			
Professional Collection			
2. Periodicals and Subscriptions:			
Print			
Online-Full Text and Abstracts			
3. Online Databases			
4. Audio			
5. Video			
6. Maps, Globes, Charts, Prints			
7. Computer:			
Software Copies			
Site Licenses			
Technical Support Fees			
8. Supplies			
Production Materials			
Other (Specify)			
9. Equipment:			
Purchase			
Repair/Replacement			
Service Contracts			
Upgrades			
10. Professional:			
Memberships			
Travel			
Professional Growth (Workshops, etc.)			
Other Professional Materials			
TOTAL EXPENDITURES PER PUPIL Expenditure for School Library Program			

Are the sources cited? Is the content primarily fact or opinion? Are the grammatical usage and spelling correct? Do multimedia elements (e.g., sound and animation) contribute to understanding the content? Does the content add to the existing body of information on the topic?

- *Authority:* Who is the creator of the Web site? What is the background/expertise of this person (or persons)? Is the author's name and e-mail address present? Is the Web site affiliated with a larger organization?

- *Navigation and Design:* Is it easy to move about the Web site? Are there discernible icons for moving through the pages and returning to the home page? Do pages load in a reasonable amount of time? Do the pages have uncluttered backgrounds with clear headings and readable fonts? (Berger 2006)

To assist with the process of evaluating Web sites, several Internet resources include sample survey forms and handout. The following sites are recommended:

Kathy Schrock's Guide for Educators: Critical Evaluation Information, http://school. discoveryeducation.com/schrockguide/eval.html

The ABCs of Web Page Evaluation (sample form), http://members.tripod.com/ bcrocke/webeval.html

The Good, the Bad, and the Ugly, http://lib.nmsu.edu/instruction/eval.html

2Learn.ca Evaluating a Website (sample forms for different grade levels), http:// www.netknowhow.ca/nkhSRevaluate.html

Joyce Valenza's WebQuest about Evaluating Websites (grades 9–12), http://www.sdst. org/shs/library/evalwebstu.html

REFERENCES

American Association of School Librarians. 2007. *AASL Standards for the 21st-Century Learner.* ALA. http.//www.ala.org/aasl/standards/.

American Association of School Librarians. *Empowering Learners: Guidelines for School Library Media Programs.* Chicago: American Library Association, 2009.

American Association of School Librarians. 2010. "Position Statements." http://www.ala.org/ ala/mgrps/divs/aasl/aaslissues/positionstatements/positionstatements.cfm.

American Library Association. 2010. *Workbook for Selection Policy Writing.* http://www.ala. org/ala/issuesadvocacy/banned/challengeslibrarymaterials/essentialpreparation/ workbookslctn/index.cfm. Available as downloadable PDF at http://www.ala.org/ala/ aboutala/offices/oif/challengesupport/dealing/workbook.pdf.

Baumbach, Donna J., and Linda L. Miller. *Less Is More: A Practical Guide to Weeding School Library Collections.* Chicago: American Library Association, 2006.

Berger, Pam. How to Evaluate Websites: For Better or Worse. *Information Searcher* 16, no. 2 (2006): 10. http://vnweb.hwwilsonweb.com/hww/results/getResults.jhtml?_DARGS=/hww/ results/results_common.jhtml.33.

Bishop, Kay. *The Collection Program in Schools: Concepts, Practices, and Information Sources.* 4th ed. Westport: Libraries Unlimited, 2007.

Kerby, Mona. *Collection Development for the School Library Media Program: A Beginner's Guide.* Chicago: American Association of School Librarians, 2006.

ADDITIONAL READINGS

Adams, Helen R. *Ensuring Intellectual Freedom and Access to Information in the School Library Media Program.* Westport: Libraries Unlimited, 2008.

Adams, Helen R. *Privacy in the 21st Century.* Westport: Libraries Unlimited, 2005.

American Association of School Librarians. *Essential Links: Resources for School Library Media Program Development: Collection Development.* http://aasl.ala.org/essentiallinks/index.php?title=Collection_Development/.

American Library Association. *Weeding Library Collections: A Selected Annotated Bibliography for Library Collection Evaluation.* http://www.ala.org/ala/aboutala/offices/library/libraryfactsheet/alalibraryfactsheet15.cfm.

Appel, Myra. *Developing Culturally Diverse Collections for the 21st Century.* Santa Barbara: Libraries Unlimited, forthcoming.

Arizona State Library. "Collection Development Training: Weeding." http://www.lib.az.us/cdt/weeding.aspx.

Cassell, Kay Ann, and Uma Hireman. *Reference and Information Services in the 21st Century.* New York: Neal-Schuman, 2010.

Dickinson, Gail. "The Challenges of Challenges: Understanding and Being Prepared (Part I)." *School Library Media Activities Monthly* 23, No. 5 (January 2007): 26–28.

Dickinson, Gail. "The Challenges of Challenges: What to Do? (Part II)." *School Library Media Activities Monthly* 23, No. 6 (February 2007): 21–24.

Dickinson, Gail. "Crying Over Spilled Milk." *Library Media Connection* 23, No. 7 (April/May 2005): 24–26.

Disher, Wayne. *Crash Course in Collection Development.* Westport: Libraries Unlimited, 2007.

Downs, Elizabeth. *The School Library Media Specialist's Policy and Procedure Writer.* New York: Neal-Schuman, 2009.

"A Guide to Handling Challenges." *School Library Media Activities Monthly* 23, No. 5 (January 2007): 2.

Harper, Meghan. *Reference Sources and Services for Youth.* New York: Neal-Schuman, 2009.

Hysell, Shannon Graff. *Recommended Reference Books for Small and Medium-Sized Libraries and Media Centers.* Santa Barbara: Libraries Unlimited, 2010.

Itner, Sheila I., Joanna F. Fountain, and Jean Weihs. *Cataloging Correctly for Kids: An Introduction to the Tools.* 5th ed. Chicago: ALA Editions, 2010.

Kaplan, Allison, and Ann Marlow Riedling. *Catalog It! A Guide to Cataloging School Library Materials.* 2nd ed. Worthington: Linworth, 2006.

Karpuk, Deborah. *KidzCat: A How-to-Do-It Manual for Cataloging Children's Materials and Instructional Resources.* New York: Neal-Schuman, 2008.

Lanning, Scott, and John Bryner. *Essential Reference Services for Today's School Media Specialists.* Santa Barbara: Libraries Unlimited, 2009.

Levine, Jenny. *Gaming and Libraries: Intersection of Services.* Chicago: ALA Editions, 2006.

Lukenbill, W. Bernard. *Community Resources in the School Library Media Center.* Westport: Libraries Unlimited, 2004.

Matthew, Kathryn I., and Joy Lowe. *The Neal-Schuman Guide to Recommended Children's Books and Media for Use with Every Elementary Subject.* 2nd ed. New York: Neal-Schuman, 2010.

Polanka, Sue. *No Shelf Required: E-Books in Libraries.* Chicago: ALA Editions, 2010.

Riedling, Ann Marlow. *Reference Skills for the School Library Media Specialist: Tools and Tips.* 2nd ed. Worthington: Linworth, 2005.

Safford, Barbara R. *Guide to Reference Materials for School Library Media Centers.* Westport: Libraries Unlimited, 2010.

Sunlink: Weed of the Month. http://www.sunlink.ucf.edu/weed/.

Texas State Library and Archives Commission. *CREW: A Weeding Manual for Modern Libraries.* http://www.tsl.state.tx.us/ld/pubs/crew/.

Weihs, Jean. *Standard Cataloging for School and Public Libraries.* Westport, CT: Libraries Unlimited, 2007.

7

School Library Facilities

RATIONALE

As a leader, information specialist, and instructional partner, the school librarian should be forward thinking in planning a physical space and environment designed to support the learning and information needs of students and teachers. The school librarian should oversee the physical arrangement of the library and should consider the following factors: size and characteristics of the school population, number of staff members, school curriculum, usage of and services provided by the school library, types of resources in the collection, materials organization, and specialized equipment and access requirements. When planning for new or renovated school library facilities, consideration should be given to the demands of the curriculum, the needs of students, and the rapid changes in technology.

This section provides a means for analyzing the physical setting of an existing school library or planning for a new or renovated and remodeled or reallocated space. There are six areas to consider in planning: flexibility, visual appeal, extended access, supervision, technology readiness, and a place for books (Baule 2007). These six areas are central to planning as well as decisions related to location, environment, space, and furnishings of the school library.

PLANNING

The school librarian needs to take a leadership role in all phases of the planning process. For a new or renovated school library facility, the school librarian will need to provide information to the architect. As the library program administrator, the school librarian is familiar with the mission, goals, and objectives of the library program and can evaluate current facilities, develop a proposal for new facilities, or provide an analysis of existing proposals for new facilities. Such input should be based on the current needs of students and teachers and should accommodate future school library program needs. The plans should also allow for input from others in the school, including administrators, teachers, and school library paraprofessionals. Others that might be included are a public librarian, school board member, regional library administrator, students, and parents. Local cable company representatives should be consulted about television distribution, and data distribution should be developed in consultation with a data network expert.

Whether the changes are large or small in scale, most renovations involve special considerations. For example, one consideration may be ensuring that the floor is structurally sound. Space to accommodate growth is another obvious concern. Oftentimes input from others on prospective changes helps to ensure that all special considerations have been included. One way to accomplish this is by involving students in the design phase by having a "redesign your library" contest (Baule 2007).

"School libraries provide equitable physical and intellectual access to the resources and tools required for learning in a warm, stimulating, and safe environment" (American Association of School Librarians [AASL] 2007). Therefore information submitted to the architect about school library space should contain the name and size of needed spaces such as circulation, reading area, instructional area, production area, reference, and technology access. Who and how many will use the spaces, an explanation of how these spaces will be used, and their relationship to each area should be included in the proposal. For example, as a teacher, the school librarian needs instructional space, and as an instructional partner, one needs space for collaboration. Also, when planning a newly constructed school, consideration must be given to placement of the school library. For example, if the center is to be open after the regular school day or in the summer, the library should be located on the main level near the front door to restrict access to the rest of the building. Access to restrooms will also need to be considered in the plans. Throughout the entire process, the school librarian must be the advocate for the school library program and the facilities needed to support it.

When working with architects, consider articulating space needs in the form of a portion of a classroom. For example, the main school library should be equal to three standard classrooms; the office and work area should be equal to half of a classroom (Baule 2007). However, designing special areas with walls that are large enough for a class should be avoided because these spaces are frequently reappropriated for other needs when space in the school becomes an issue (Hart 2006). Story pits are a consideration for an elementary school library; however, they can become a problem from a safety standpoint (Baule 2007).

As stated in *Empowering Learners*, "the school library media program includes flexible and equitable access to physical and virtual collections of resources that support the school curriculum and meet the diverse needs of all learners" (AASL 2009, 33). Therefore facilities must be planned for future growth and change by asking the following questions: what technology will be needed in the future? How many books, electronic media, and equipment will be added? Will distance education equipment be required? How will school library functions expand and change? Will more classes utilize social networking and other individual communication tools? Is the school population expected to grow? Will more than one class be using the school library at one time? What is the teaching style of the school librarian? What method of teaching is being used, inquiry or problem based?

One must also ask what the school librarian can do to provide for a learning space. In *Empowering Learners: Guidelines for School Library Media Programs* (AASL 2009), the following are given as suggested actions:

- creates an environment that is conducive to active and participatory learning, resource-based learning, and collaboration with teaching staff
- ensures that library hours provide optimum access for learners and other members of the school community
- promotes flexible scheduling of the school library facility to allow for efficient and timely integration of resources into the curriculum
- creates a friendly, comfortable, well-lit, aesthetically pleasing, and ergonomic space that is centrally located and well integrated with the rest of the school
- designs learning spaces that accommodate a range of teaching methods, learning tasks, and learning outcomes
- provides space and seating that enhances and encourages technology use, leisure reading and browsing, and use of materials in all formats
- provides sufficient and appropriate shelving and storage of resources
- designs and maintains a library Web site that provides 24-7 access to digital information resources, instructional interventions references, links to other libraries and academic sites, information for parents, and exhibits of exemplary student work
- ensures that technology and telecommunications infrastructure is adequate to support teaching and learning (AASL 2009, 33)

Excerpted from *Empowering Learners: Guidelines for School Library Media Programs*, by the American Association of School Librarians, a division of the American Library Association, copyright © 2009, American Library Association. Used with permission.

Special needs, such as wiring, built-in equipment, security, storage, and environment (lighting, carpeting, ventilation, temperature, etc.), should be noted. These needs must be considered for the entire school library as well as for individual spaces. A list should be made of the movable furniture and equipment needed in the facilities. To assist in the evaluation of furnishings, standard dimensions and types of furnishings needed in a school library have been included in the "Furnishings" section; recommended spacing for furnishings is also included. In evaluating a planned school library and the furnishings, current Americans with Disabilities Act regulations must be consulted.

PARTNERING WITH PUBLIC LIBRARY FACILITIES

The trend toward joint use of library facilities may grow as tax-supported institutions experience budget difficulties. If a joint-use facility is being considered, there are many things to be considered and discussed before entering into a formal arrangement. While superintendents and mayors or city administrators have the authority to enter into partnership agreements, library staff from both the school and public sides should be involved in discussions prior to planning any merger or joint building project.

A primary consideration for the school community will be security, especially if there are plans to have the library open to the public during the school day. Separate entrances for the public and the school should be considered, and the children's section and instructional area should be located away from the public entrance and adult areas. There may be a need to have separate restrooms in the children's section that are not accessible to adults. If a decision is made to restrict public access to the children's section and instructional areas during the school day, this will have to be carefully planned to maintain visibility and access to the children's collection when the area is used during nonschool time.

Public input during the planning process is critical so that concerns can be aired and addressed regarding security measures. There should be a joint safety plan so that staff respond to emergencies such as a tornado or intruder in a coordinated way. The government entities will need to enter into a contractual arrangement that spells out the specifics of percentages of payment for the building, utilities, maintenance, collection development and management, technology and network costs, and staff. In addition, the cooperating entities may wish to include in the contract when the public and school patrons have access to the various areas of the library. For example, a community room may be considered joint-use space that is only accessible for school use during the day. If a school group such as a parent organization wishes to use that space after school hours, it would have to book it through the public library side.

This type of joint-use facility should not be attempted if existing staff are unable to work collaboratively to make it a success. When selecting new staff, individuals should be chosen who are flexible and have strong communication skills. There are dozens of failed joint-use libraries, and the typical reason they fail is staff conflict. The missions of the school and public library are different, and both entities should enter into the agreement with a strong commitment to make the arrangement work. Because personnel will change, it is important to have a jointly prepared vision statement that can be presented to possible candidates so they have a clear understanding of the facility's purpose. An example of such a vision statement from a joint-use project that was constructed and opened in Omaha in 2009 follows:

The Saddlebrook shared venture, consisting of Omaha Public Schools, Omaha Public Library, and the Omaha Parks and Recreation Department, is a vital and active community resource known for its innovative programs, customer-centered focus, and visionary leadership. Belief statements:

- All parties are enthusiastic and dedicated to the long-term success of the shared facility.
- Each organization will make staffing decisions based upon a commitment to the shared vision.
- The entities will target the needs of current and prospective users in order to engage and connect them with resources, services and opportunities.
- All entities shall strive to use resources in effective and efficient ways.
- All patrons who follow facility rules will be made welcome in any area of the facility.
- Each organization will provide continuing financial support similar to that which is provided in other stand alone facilities.

- The joint use space is to be shared and cooperation in scheduling is expected.
- Regular and open communication among all staff employed by the entities will be necessary to the successful operation. Formal meetings of site management will take place on a regularly scheduled basis with the school management responsible for scheduling the meetings.
- All entities will strive to maintain a safe environment for library and rec center patrons, and staff, students, and visitors to the school. A crisis plan will be developed involving all three entities to ensure that response to an emergency situation is well coordinated.
- All entities will agree on a common code of conduct for patrons of the facility. A common ban and bar process will be developed and honored by all entities (Omaha Public Schools, Omaha Public Library, and Omaha Parks and Recreation Department 2008)

The following tables are suggestions for location, space allocation, environment, and furnishings for new or renovated facilities. Since school libraries are flexible and evolving, these tables and rubrics may be used to assist in identifying facility updates as the school library program changes.

Table 7.1

A. Location	What We Have	What We Need
1. The school library is located conveniently and centrally in relation to other learning areas. Consider: Proximity to noisy areas, inconveniences, distances, floor levels, building construction, etc. 2. The loading and delivery areas are convenient to the school library. Consider: Inconveniences, distances, stairs, elevators, external door, etc. 3. The school library is readily accessible to faculty work areas. 4. The location of the school library permits outside accessibility for extended hours. Consider: Restroom accessibility, building security, emergency exits, etc. 5. The school library is located such that security can be maintained after school hours. 6. The school library is easily accessible to the handicapped. Consider: Ease of access, entrances and exits, signage, ramps, elevators, and restrooms		

Table 7.2

B. Space Allocation	What We Have	What We Need

1. Main Area: One Large Room
Consider:
Flexibility to allow for multiple activities and changes in curriculum and technology.
Have ease of supervision. Provide clear flow of traffic (Maine 1999).
Activities occurring in the school library: What equipment is needed? What storage is needed? How many students will use it at one time? Can the space seat at least one class, plus some small (teaching) groups and individuals?
Possible Areas:
  a. Circulation
  b. Reading area Soft furniture, heavy enough that students can't move
  c. Computer information retrieval online catalog, databases
  d. Instruction: equipped for presentations using different media, near reference
  e. Plan 36 square feet per 42" table with 4 chairs (Baule 2007).
  f. Shelving for materials: reference, fiction, nonfiction, picture books, biographies
  g. Computers for student use and scanner
  h. Small and large group (teaching) activities
2. Work Area
Consider:
  a. School librarian: enclosed office to confer with teachers, telephone, telecommunications, visual access to student area, locked storage.
  b. Paraprofessionals: near entrance and circulation. Provision for storage of supplies, water, several outlets, telephone, telecommunications, counters and /or tables for work area to unpack new materials, hold books for mending, visual access to student area.
  c. Equipment maintenance and repair: near loading dock, elevator, corridor, secure, included workbench with electrical outlets and telecommunications, telephone, storage.
  d. Media distribution: Taping offline and TV, in school video distribution, storage for equipment and supplies.
  e. Place to store coats.
3. Equipment storage
Consider:
Near corridor, elevator and main area, secure area, electrical outlets, telecommunications, telephone, shelves, pegboard.
  a. Store and charge mobile laptops and computers
  b. Excellent lighting		

Table 7.2

B. Space Allocation	What We Have	What We Need

c. Counter space for charging batteries
   d. Locked cabinetry
   e. Small bins or drawers for bulbs and small equipment
   f. Open shelving for large equipment
   g. Repair space		

4. Entrance Consider: One entrance is best, 500–600 square feet if have separate exit and entrance (Baule 2007).		
5. Network and Server Consider: High security, central in building, adequate lighting, ventilation, temperature control, space to be serviced (Baule 2007).		
6. Other areas Consider: Production and distribution with sink and water Production area for teachers and/or students Dark room Television studio Audio studio Telecommunications distribution Periodical storage Conference rooms Teacher/professional area Computer lab		

Table 7.3

C. Environment	What We Have	What We Need
1. Lighting specified according to tasks. Consider: Need for zoned and controlled dimmer switches, blackout options, diffused light, placement of lights to eliminate shadows, controls in an easily accessible central location, a need to turn lights on and off in more than one place.		
2. Year-round temperature and humidity controls for optimum operation and storage conditions. Consider: Relative humidity of 40% for computers. Humidity above 60% can result in damaged books and paper jams in copy machines (Baule, 2007). Temperature should not vary more than 12 degrees throughout the year, using 65 degrees Fahrenheit as a base (Baule, 2007).		
3. Acoustical treatment: Consider: Think of noise from the outside, equipment, students. Treat floors, walls, and ceilings. Isolate noisy areas.		
4. Electrical power, outlets, and telecommunication Consider: Activities in the school library and where multiple electrical outlets (floor or wall and how high) are needed, where multiple telecommunications hookups need to be and near TV, phone placement. Surge protection, isolated ground, dedicated circuits, interference, intercom, carrels, raceways for future growth, etc. Outlets for students to charge their own laptops.		
5. Appearance and aesthetics Consider: Use of space, arrangements, acoustics, furnishings, color, texture, carpeting, display areas, etc.		
6. Arrangement of the center Consider: Functionality and efficiency in terms of work flow, traffic flow, and supervision. Meets ADA requirements for space width. Recommendations: 3 feet between rows of shelves 5 feet between shelves and furniture involving seating 5 feet between two tables with back-to-back seating 3 feet between tables and walls or between ends of shelves and the furniture that does not involve seating 4 feet between table ends and rows of shelves		

Table 7.4

D. Furnishings	What We Have	What We Need
1. Seating: Consider: Appropriate to size and age of students and to activities. Upholstered or not? Fire retardant? Regular legs or sled base? Stackable? ADA requirements met? Recommendations: Standard chairs: Elementary: Height: 14–17 inches Junior High/Middle School: Height: 16–18 inches High School: Height: 16–18 inches (Wisconsin Department of Education [WDE] 2006) Staff: Secretarial-type chair Circulation: Secretarial-type chair or stool Computer chairs: Adjustable in height Wheels or no wheels		
2. Tables: Consider: Height for size and age of students and to activities. Types of projects to be completed. Other functions held in the school library. Washable tops. Square table allow for rearranging and moving together. One more table than necessary for largest class so teacher can confer with students. Recommendation: Elementary: Height: 24–28 inches Width: 3 feet Length: 5–6 feet Round: 4 feet in diameter Square: 48 inches per side Junior High/Middle School Height: 27–30 inches Width: 3 feet Length: 5–6 feet Round: 4 feet in diameter Square: 48 inches per side		

(Continued)

Table 7.4

D. Furnishings	What We Have	What We Need
High School Height: 29–30 inches Width: 3 feet Length: 5–6 feet Round: 4 feet in diameter Square: 48 inches per side Workroom/staff Height: 29–30 inches Width: 3 feet Length: 5–6 feet Round: 4 feet in diameter Square: 48 inches per side		
3. Listening and Viewing Stations: For both individual and group work. Consider: Computer workstations: Adjustable in height. Allow 30 square feet per workstation (WDE 2006). Provide space for students to lay books and write. Wireless. Carrels: With or without electricity. Recommendations: Depth: 24 inches Height: 25–29 inches (depending on elementary or high school) Width: 36 inches		
4. Shelving: Consider: Room for expansion. Shelves no more than two-thirds full. To determine size for collection, multiply number of books by number of titles needed per student. Adjustable. Have backing and ends. Suitable for types of material being stored (paperbacks, A-V, picture books, globes, open, closed, periodicals). Double faced or single. On rollers. Plan for some office and work areas and perhaps a storage area. Recommendation: A Capacity estimates of shelving: Number of books per three foot shelf when two-thirds full: Books of average size: 30 Reference books: 18 Picture books: 60 (WDE 2006)		

Table 7.4

D. Furnishings	What We Have	What We Need
B. Width of section on centers: 3 feet Depth of shelving: Standard: 8–10 inches Oversized: 10–15 inches Picture books: 12 inches Periodicals: slanting shelves: 16 inches straight shelves: 14–16 inches storage of: 12–15 inches Adjustable Thickness of shelves: 1 inch approximate. Gauge of steel shelving: 18 gauge minimum. Height of section: Base: 4–6 inches total height of standard section: Elementary: 42 or 48 inches Junior High/Middle School: 5–6 feet High School: 5–6 feet Staff: 5–6 feet Storage: up to 82 inches depending on what is stored. G. Spacing of shelves: Between stacks: minimum of 36 inches		
5. Other Furnishings: A. Books trucks (circulation and staff workroom) B. Circulation desk with book drop Elementary: desk height Secondary: counter height C. Card catalog (if not automated): Capacity estimate: 6 cards per item, 1,000 cards per drawer. Appropriate height for students. Add-on units for growth. D. Casual seating E. Desks (for staff) F. Dictionary stand G. Display boards H. Electronic control system (theft security). Some are affected by computers, photocopiers and some lighting ballasts. I. Exhibit cases J. Large picture files K. Legal-size file cabinets (media center and staff) L. Write-on boards M. Step stools (staff, storage)		

(Continued)

Table 7.4

D. Furnishings	What We Have	What We Need
6. Equipment: A. Carts: appropriate for type of equipment, with or without electrical cord B. Computers Consider: Hardware requirements of the software and backup for online catalog and circulation Recommendations: A. Computers: One computer per 100 students for the online catalog. One for each staff person. Some for individual student use. Enough for a class if no computer lab. B. Mobile cart with laptops C. Copy machines D. Interactive white boards E. LCD projectors F. Power surge protectors G. Printers H. Slip printers for circulation I. Uninterrupted power supply for at least a server		
7. Communications: A. Telephone: Consider: Near circulation, near computer server, staff offices, teacher work area. Staff offices need long distance access. B. Internet access C. Online circulation and catalog D. Raceways E. Wireless access points		
8. Walls and Windows: A. Walls: Consider: Color of paint: pleasing and generally a background. Bright primary colors for elementary. Tints of blue, green, gray, and beige for secondary (Baule 2007). Is soundproofing necessary? B. Windows: Consider: What type of window covering is needed? Do you want or need skylights? Will you need to cover them? Do you need black-out shades? Windows at least 45 inches from the floor to allow for standard 42 inch shelving.		

Table 7.4

D. Furnishings	What We Have	What We Need
9. Floors: Consider areas of activity. Carpeting in main area for sound control. Carpet tile for raceway area. Tile in storage and workroom.		
10. Storage: Consider: Built-in cupboards, closets, and drawers designed for what is stored there, e.g., equipment. Space for large and small equipment and carts. Space for storing and charging laptop carts. Recommendation: Total height of counter section: 42 inches		
11. Lighting and power outlets: Consider: Location of main light controls. Do you want to be able to turn off certain lights and leave the others on? How will you deal with glare form overhead lights? Wall and floor outlets and placement in room, including circulation desk.		
12. Signage: A. Directional: where to go for services or resources. Entrance and exit. Manage traffic flow. B. Location: circulation desk, reference area, copy machine, story area. C. Rooms: where to go in room, staff only, school library office, conference room (Baule 2007).		

Table 7.5 Facility Rubric

Area	Excellent	Acceptable	Needs Improvement	Unacceptable
Location	All items listed under Acceptable, plus near front entrance and near restrooms.	Easy access for all students. Accessible after school hours. One entrance.	A few students have to come a long way. Difficult access after school hours.	Multiple entrances, near noisy activities. Away from main entrance. Two floors. School library used as hallway.
Environment	All items listed under Acceptable, plus has separate heating and air-conditioning controls. Sound proofing on walls. Zone lighting with controls near area where used. Voice amplification. Sink for student use.	Temperature and humidity appropriate for resources and equipment. Lighting adequate for all activities in school library. Carpeting, appropriate color for age of students. Sink for staff use.	Temperature and humidity to high or low for resources and equipment. Blinds do not block light, paint needs updating, carpet worn.	No humidity control. Sound echoes in room. Colors dark and drab. Lighting cannot be controlled. No access to water. Light switch opposite wall from door.
Space	All items listed under Acceptable, plus space to seat two classes at the same time and individual student use. Conference rooms, other rooms to support learning such as darkrooms and production areas. Professional library.	Adequate for number of students needed to use school library at same time. Flexibility in use. Good traffic flow. Space for various activities carried out in school library. Office for school librarian and work space for library paraprofessional.	Adding a new service will require major rearrangement. Some minor problems with traffic flow. School librarian and library paraprofessional share same work space.	Classroom sized. No room to expand service. Columns block line of sight. Little flexibility in school library arrangement. Traffic flow problems. No work space for school librarian or library paraprofessional.
Furnishings	All items listed under Acceptable, plus room for collection to grow. Reading area for students. Interactive white boards.	Correct size and height for students. Sufficient computers for student and staff work. Adequate for shelving	Furnishings worn. Phones for intercom use only. Computers need updating.	Furnishings incorrect height and size for students or in poor condition. Shelves built into walls.

Table 7.5 Facility Rubric (*Continued*)

Area	Excellent	Acceptable	Needs Improvement	Unacceptable
		collection and equipment. Phones for staff with long-distance access.		
Handicap accessibility	Provides accommodations above those required by ADA.	Meets ADA requirements for SLMC space, shelving, furnishings, signage, sinks, environment, flooring, accessibility.	Meets some but not all of the ADA requirements for school libraries.	Meets few if any ADA requirements for school libraries.

Adapted to *Empowering Learners: Guidelines for School Library Programs* (by the American Association of School Librarians, a division of the American Library Association, copyright © 2009 American Library Association). Used with permission.

REFERENCES

American Association of School Librarians. 2007. *AASL Standards for the 21st-Century Learner*. http://www.ala.org/aasl/standards/.

American Association of School Librarians. *Empowering Learners: Guidelines for School Library Media Programs*. Chicago: American Library Association, 2009.

Baule, Steve M. *Facility Planning for School Media and Technology Centers*. 2nd ed. Columbus: Linworth, 2007.

Hart, Thomas L. *The School Library Media Facilities Planner*. New York: Neal-Schuman, 2006.

Omaha Public Schools, Omaha Public Library, and Omaha Parks and Recreation Department. 2008. "Saddlebrook Shared Venture: Belief Statements."

ADDITIONAL READINGS

American Association of School Librarians. *Empowering Learners: Guidelines for School Library Media Programs*. Chicago: American Library Association, 2009.

American Association of School Librarians. *Standards for the 21st-Century Learner*. Chicago: American Library Association, 2007.

Anderson, Mary Alice. "Fighting the Good Fight: Designing a Library Media Center." *Book Report* 20, No. 1 (2001): 6–9.

Baule, Steve M. "Planning Considerations for Library Media Center Facilities." *Book Report* 24, No. 3 (2005): 14–15.

Erikson, Rolf, and Carolyn Markuson. *Designing a School Library Media Center for the Future.* 2nd ed. Chicago: American Association of School Libraries, 2007.

Farrelly, Michael G. *Make Room for Teens! A Guide to Developing Teen Spaces in the Library.* Santa Barbara: Libraries Unlimited, 2010.

Fortriede, Steven Carl. *Moving Your Library: Getting the Collection from Here to There.* Chicago: ALA Editions, 2010.

Habich, Elizabeth Chamberlain. *Moving Library Collections.* Santa Barbara: Libraries Unlimited, 2009.

Hart, Thomas L. "Do You Really Want Your Library Media Center Used?" *Book Report* 24, No. 3 (2005): 16–19.

Johnson, Doug. *Some Design Considerations.* http://www.doug-johnson.com/dougwri/some-design-considerations.htm.

Lushington, Nolan. *Libraries Designed for Kids.* New York: Neal-Schuman, 2008.

Maine Association of School Librarians. 1999. *Maine School Library Facilities Handbook: General Considerations.* http://www.maslibraries.org/resources/pubs/facilities/index.html.

Massachusetts School Library Media Association. Massachusetts School Library Media Program Standard Information (Access and Delivery for Students Learning: Facilities Standards). 2003 (pages 15–19). http://www.maschoolibraries.org/dmdocuments/standardsrev.pdf.

Miller, Joseph. *Internet Technologies and Information Services.* Westport: Libraries Unlimited, 2008.

Moyer, Mary, and Rosalie M. Baker. "Re-designing a School Library Media Center for the 21st Century." *Book Report* 22, No. 7 (2004): 24–25.

Thomas, M.J.K. *Re-designing the High School Library for the Forgotten Half: Information Needs of the Non-college Bound Students.* Westport: Libraries Unlimited, 2008.

U.S. Department of Justice. 2002. *ADA Standards for Accessible Design.* http://www.ada.gov/stds pdf.htm.

Wisconsin Department of Education. 2006. *Design Considerations for School Library Media Centers.* http://dpi.state.wi.us.imt/desgnlmc.html.

Index